ALL-IRELAND AMBITIONS

JOHN SCALLY is the author of the bestselling biographies, *Dermot Earley, The Earley Years* and *Tony Ward, The Good, the Bad and the Rugby*

To unsung heroes of the GAA everywhere,
but particularly in memory of the late Peadar Earley.

ACKNOWLEDGEMENTS

My sincere thanks to Ciaran Barr, Mick Bermingham, Seamus Bonner, Eddie Boyle, Marie Brady, Padraig Brogan, Mick Carley, Dessie Donnelly, Joe Dooley, Mick Dunne, Pat Dunphy, Dermot Earley, Jim Fives, Jimmy Flynn, Mick Galwey, Micheál Herbert, Johnny Hughes, Nudie Hughes, Michael Kearins, Eddie Keher, Kevin Kehilly, Stephen King, Gary Kirby, Maureen McAleenan, Eilish McCabe, Packy McGarty, Willie McGee, Peter McGinnity, Oliver McHugh, Jim McKeever, John McKnight, Jimmy Magee, Pat Mangan, Frances Morley, Jimmy Murray, Willie Nolan, Gay O'Driscoll, Mícheál Ó Muircheartaigh, Gerry O'Reilly, Jack O'Shea, Billy Quinn, Martin Quigley, Paddy Quirke, Ken Rennicks, Sue Ramsbottom, Seamus Scally and Jimmy Smyth for their time, generosity and insights.

I am grateful to my good friends Brian Carthy and Peter Woods for their interest in my work and for their many kindnesses to me in recent years.

ALL-IRELAND AMBITIONS

JOHN SCALLY

WOLFHOUND PRESS

Published in 2001 by
Wolfhound Press Ltd
68 Mountjoy Square
Dublin 1, Ireland
Tel: (353-1) 874 0354
Fax: (353-1) 872 0207

British Library Cataloguing in Publication Data
A catalogue record for this book is available from the British Library.

ISBN 0-86327-827-2

10 9 8 7 6 5 4 3 2 1

Cover photographs: Courtesy of Inpho Photography
Photographs of players courtesy of interviewees and their families
Cover Design: Azure Design
Typesetting and book design: Wolfhound Press
Printed in the Republic of Ireland by ColourBooks, Dublin

Contents

Introduction   7

Pint of View   9
A Hurling Dynasty in the Green Glens of Antrim   14
Captain Fantastic   21
Hurling in the Congo   26
Licence to Thrill   32
The Star of the County Down   37
The Purple and Gold   42
The Mighty Quinn   50
Quirke of Fate   57
The Man from Clare   63
Famous Seamus   69
The Prince of Full-Backs   77
The Day the Crossbar Broke   82
The Player   88
Midfield Maestro   93
Thy Kingdom Come   102
On a Wing and a Player   109
Nudie   117
Keeping up with Jones   123
Lethal Weapon   129
Elation Once Again   134

King Stephen   139

Amongst Lilywhites   144

Super Mac   151

On Guard   159

Prince among Thoroughbreds   166

Jim'll Fix It   172

McKnight Moves   177

Jeepers Keepers   182

O'Reilly: Ace of Fives   187

Captain Marvel   192

Pride and Passion   198

In the Line of Duty   201

Appendices   205

    1: Wired for Sound   207

    2: Lest We Forget   212

    3: It Could Happen to a Bishop   218

INTRODUCTION

In the rich history of the GAA, many great players who dreamed of winning an All-Ireland medal never had their hopes fulfilled. But while they may not have reached the peak of their personal ambitions, they made a magnificent contribution to Gaelic games nonetheless. This book is a tribute to those players.

My most difficult task was to decide which of them to feature, and I am acutely aware that many people will not agree with all of my choices. I have tried to serve the reader by compiling a diverse range of personal profiles, drawing in players from different eras and positions on the pitch, and getting a good mix of personalities. I also wanted to give each county representation. And in keeping with the richly deserved success of ladies' football and camogie in recent years, I opted to feature one player from each of these codes.

Broadly speaking, I applied three criteria when making my final selection. The players had to have a long playing career, with consistently outstanding displays in all competitions but especially on the 'big day'. They must be highly committed and motivated, and display a high level of sportsmanship on the field.

My starting point was the 1984 *Sunday Independent*/Irish Nationwide/GAA Teams of the Century, selected by a special panel, after the *Sunday Independent* had carried out a national poll of its readers, and made up of players who had never won an All-Ireland senior championship medal. For the record, those teams were:

Hurling: Sean Duggan (Galway), Jim Fives (Waterford), Noel Drumgoole (Dublin), J.J. Doyle (Clare), Sean Herbert (Limerick),

Sean Stack (Clare), Colm Doran (Wexford), Joe Salmon (Galway), 'Jobber' McGrath (Westmeath), Josie Gallagher (Galway), Martin Quigley (Wexford), Kevin Armstrong (Antrim), Jimmy Smyth (Clare), Christy O'Brien (Laois), Mick Bermingham (Dublin).

Football: Aidan Brady (Roscommon), Willie Casey (Mayo), Eddie Boyle (Louth), John McKnight (Armagh), Gerry O'Reilly (Wicklow), Gerry O'Malley (Roscommon), Sean Quinn (Armagh), Jim McKeever (Derry), Tommy Murphy (Laois), Sean O'Connell (Derry), Packy McGarty (Leitrim), Michael Kearins (Sligo), Charlie Gallagher (Cavan), Willie McGee (Mayo), Dinny Allen (Cork).

While this gave me a good benchmark it also restricted my options, as a number of counties had more than one player on the teams. Moreover, some of these men had passed to their eternal reward, while an interview-driven book by definition focuses on the living. However, I felt it important to recognise some players who were no longer with us. In the case of the late Aidan Brady, I publish for the first time his final interview before his death.

Kerry gave me the most selection headaches, as all its great players have multiple All-Ireland medals. I cheated somewhat by choosing Mick Galwey as my representative from the Kingdom. He never got to play in an All-Ireland final, even though he won an All-Ireland medal from the subs' bench in 1986.

In honouring the greatest players never to win an All-Ireland medal, I also felt it appropriate to honour the unsung heroes of the GAA: the players, mentors and the fans. For this reason I include in the Appendices a representative of each. The late John Morley and Aidan McAnespie personify the many quiet heroes found in every parish in the country who dedicate so much to the GAA, while Bishop Willie Walsh represents the finest of the many mentors without whom Gaelic games would cease to exist. I also wanted to honour a man in this category who has dedicated his whole working life to the GAA, but who has not always received the recognition he deserves — one of the voices of Gaelic games, Mick Dunne.

PINT OF VIEW

Mick Bermingham's career with Dublin spanned four decades, from his debut in senior inter-county hurling as a sixteen-year-old in 1959, to his last game at intermediate level in 1982. He enjoyed great success with Leinster, winning six Railway Cup medals, including a four-in-a-row in 1971–74, and in 1971 he was selected at right corner-forward on the inaugural All-Stars. In 1984 he was chosen at left corner-forward on the centenary team of greatest players never to have won an All-Ireland final.

Additional achievements include ten senior club championship medals, the highlight coming when he captained Kilmacud Crokes

Mick Bermingham, with a hurley at his toe, is poised for the breaking ball.

to win the Dublin title. Mick considers this side unlucky not to have won a Leinster club title. He was also a prolific scorer for Kilmacud Crokes in the All-Ireland sevens competition.

Bermingham had an impressive family lineage.

I had hurling on both sides of the family. My mother's brother, Paddy Ford, played full-back in the 1947 Connacht Railway Cup side that beat Munster. My father's first cousin, 'young' Mick Gill, was on the Dublin side that won the 1938 All-Ireland.

However, Bermingham himself was denied the opportunity to perform on the highest stage.

In 1961 I broke a few fingers in a club match and I missed out on the chance to play for Dublin in the All-Ireland. It was agonising to watch the Leinster final, let alone the All-Ireland final. Dublin lost to Tipperary on a scoreline of 1–12 to 0–16, but we could have won. We had a lean year in 1962 and qualified for the Leinster finals in both 1963 and 1964, only to lose to a Kilkenny side who went on to have fifteen years of great success.

For me, consolation came in the Railway Cups, which were massive back then.

Listening to Bermingham talk, one can hear the roar of the crowd, the whirr of the sliotar flying, and the thrilling clash of ash against ash. One of his best moments came in 1964, when Dublin scored a shock win over Kilkenny in the Walsh Cup final in Nowlan Park by 5–4 to 2–12. Bermingham was the hero of the hour, scoring 4–3 of his side's total despite receiving an injury which forced him to retire for a spell. He had the ball in the Kilkenny net twice in the opening two minutes, the first goal coming from a free and the second in the mêlée which caused his injury. However, the corner-forward was back before half-time and went on to score two further goals and three points. His last point proved to be a winner.

The match had a comical sequel.

I didn't know it at the time, but I had dislocated my shoulder. Des Ferguson was over the team and asked me if I could go back. I was patched up again and took my place, but the circulation went out of my arms and my shoulder was paralysed after the match.

There was great jubilation in the dressing-room because beating Kilkenny was like winning the Leinster final. However, I was having great, great difficulty changing my clothes. When I came back from having a shower our dressing-room was empty, and then, as I finished dressing, I found that some so-and-so had tied my shoelaces together!

When Limerick played Kilkenny in the 1940 final, the legendary Mick Mackey turned at the edge of the square after his opening shot was saved by goalkeeper Jimmy O'Connell, and shouted: 'You're in good form, but you won't smell the next one!' Bermingham had a similar rivalry with Kilkenny goalie Ollie Walsh, and for him the victory over Kilkenny was particularly sweet. His best match, however, was one he played for Leinster.

When we beat Munster in the Railway Cup final for my first medal, I couldn't believe how excited the great Kilkenny and Wexford players were. They were legends of the game and multiple All-Ireland medal-winners, but they were like children because they hadn't won the Railway Cup before. I had an exceptional day. I was on John Doyle, a giant of the game, and I was only a nipper from Dublin. Coming out of the dressing-room another of the hurling immortals, Jimmy Langton of Kilkenny, came up to me and congratulated me on how well I played. That meant a lot.

The formative influences on Bermingham's career were his father and John Howard.

I met John for the first time when I was twelve. It was he who drew me into hurling and joining Kilmacud Crokes. He got a group of young lads together and did a great job with us. After that, things took off for me.

I can't describe what he meant to me. When John died, it was a huge loss — I lost interest in hurling for a while and went to America.

Some forty years later, Mick is overcome with emotion when recalling John Howard's death, and for a few minutes I switch off the tape.

While Bermingham was away, Dublin lost the 1967 All-Ireland under-21 final to Tipperary, beaten by a point in the last minute by John Flanagan. In New York, Bermingham played for Galway 'because of the family connection,' and resumed his career with Dublin when he came back in 1970. They won the Leinster intermediate championship, beating Kilkenny in the final. '1971 was a particularly good year for me in the scoring stakes,' Bermingham recalls. It was also a lively period for the county.

Dublin had won the minor All-Ireland in 1965 and seven or eight of them had come through, so things started to move with the senior team. Kilkenny beat us in the Leinster semi-final two years — they were at their peak then — and in 1974 we got to the league semi-final but Cork beat us by a point. They went on to hammer the reigning All-Ireland champions, Limerick, in the final, and to win three All-Irelands. So although we never got there, we were thereabouts.

Which player did he most admire?

It has to be Christy Ring. I first got to know him when he was working in Dublin and used go training in Islandbridge. I was fifteen and he was in the autumn of his career. My uncle played against him in the Railway Cup final in 1947, and that gave me the courage to go up and speak to him. We pucked a few balls together.

I got to know him better when I played with him in the Cardinal Cushing games in America. He was very intense. There were no short-cuts with him. It was an education to watch him. He had great antici-pation and was a master of judging the flight of the sliotar.

I learned a lot about how to play corner-forward from him. If he got a score he'd dance a little jig to annoy his opponent, and straight away won the psychological battle. I always tried to out-think my opponent and never stood still in a match.

Bermingham worked in the bar business, and the continual anti-social hours were an impediment to his career. His job came back to haunt him in a memorable moment on the hurling field during the 1963 Leinster final against Kilkenny.

It was a lovely sunny day and I was the free-taker. At the time a friend of mine was working on a luxury liner and he asked the captain if he could listen to the match on the ship's radio. In fact, he talked my skills up so much that the captain decided to listen in with him. Mícheál O'Hehir had been praising me in his commentary so my friend was feeling totally vindicated, and then we got a free into the Canal End goal. Mícheál said something like, 'The diminutive Mick Bermingham is about to take a free for Dublin and this will surely be a point,' but when I was lifting the ball it tilted away from me and I put it wide. The captain turned to my friend and said, 'He wasn't much of a hero there.'

When I ran back into the corner after the free, I heard a Dublin voice ringing out clearly among the 40,000 crowd. He said, 'Ah sure, Bermingham, you can't score a point, and what's worse, you can't fuckin' even pull a pint!'

Mick Bermingham's dream team is as follows:

Ollie Walsh (Kilkenny)
Fan Larkin (Kilkenny) Nick O'Donnell (Wexford) Tom Neville (Wexford)
Mick Roche (Tipperary) Pat Henderson (Kilkenny) Martin Coogan (Kilkenny)
John Connolly (Galway) Frank Cummins (Kilkenny)
Jimmy Doyle (Tipperary) Des Foley (Dublin) Eddie Keher (Kilkenny)
Christy Ring (Cork) Tony Doran (Wexford) Eamonn Cregan (Limerick)

A HURLING DYNASTY
IN THE GREEN GLENS OF ANTRIM

The Donnelly clan from Ballycastle are the most famous dynasty in Antrim hurling. In 1907 Edward Donnelly co-founded the Ballycastle McQuillans Club and was its first chairman. In 1989 his great-great-grandson, Dessie Donnelly, won an All-Star at left full-back for a commanding performance which carried Antrim to the All-Ireland final that year.

Dessie's team-mates included his brother, Brian, and cousin, Terry, son of the legendary 'Bear' Donnelly, who hurled with distinction for club and county in the fifties and sixties. His older brother, Eddie, won a record eight Antrim Senior Hurling Championship medals with Ballycastle, and in 1970 won both a National League (Division 2) medal and an All-Ireland Intermediate Championship. He played in two shinty internationals and went to the USA as a replacement All-Star in both 1975 and 1977. Another brother, Kevin, also played for Antrim hurlers.

'Hurling seems to be in our genes,' Dessie Donnelly remarks.

I think I was given a hurley in my hand as soon as I could walk! At that stage we were being dragged along to matches, so our hurling education began before any other type of education. Now my son plays for the club, as do my brothers' sons. It looks like the future for the Donnellys in hurling is secure.

'When all is said and done, blood is thicker than water,' he says. He recollects the highlights of his career, 'representing Ballycastle at the Féile na Gael in 1971, winning my first senior Antrim championship in 1975 as a sixteen-year-old, winning three All-Ireland B championships with Antrim in 1978, 1981 and 1982.' But the absolute highlight 'was winning an All-Ireland B final with three of my brothers — Brian, Kevin and Eddie — also on the team. That was even more special than our famous victory over Offaly in 1989.'

In 1978, when Derry rock band The Undertones were singing about 'Teenage Kicks', the teenage Dessie Donnelly's life revolved around hurling.

In 1977, when I was still a minor, I made my senior debut for Antrim. I came on as a sub in a league match against Westmeath in Mullingar. I scored a point and held my place after that.

He and his brothers were more than holding their places with their home club, Ballycastle, which reached the All-Ireland Senior Hurling Club Final in 1980. They lost the title to Castlegar of Galway in a game which is still vivid in Dessie Donnelly's memory twenty years on. He recalls:

The match was billed as the clash between the Connollys and the Donnellys, because there were seven Connollys playing for Castlegar and seven Donnellys playing for us. We really thought we could do it and it was a crushing blow when we lost. That was the biggest disappointment of my career — even more so than losing the All-Ireland to Tipperary, because no one really expected us to win in 1989. It was very different in 1980.

Dessie Donnelly takes a free.

But the 1980s also offered Donnelly some of his most satisfying moments in sport.

I was first nominated for the All-Stars in 1986. Although I didn't get selected I was chosen as a replacement for the trip to America in 1987, which is the nicest consolation prize I ever got for anything. To be selected on the actual team in 1989 was, I'd say, the biggest thrill I ever got in hurling. I can't explain in words just how much it meant.

The year 1989 also presented Donnelly with his sole opportunity to play on the highest stage in the game. All that stood between him and an All-Ireland final was a semi-final clash with Offaly. Just over a week previously Galway had hammered Antrim in a challenge match, suggesting to neutrals that the Northerners would be like lambs to the slaughter in the semi-final, but Antrim's confidence was high because they had already beaten Offaly twice that year. All-Ireland semi-final or not, the men in saffron and white thought of it simply as a game against Offaly, and were mentally right for the match.

From the whistle, Offaly made the better start and their half-time lead was 1–10 to 1–6. But it was a different story in the second half, as Dessie Donnelly marshalled the Antrim defence superbly and Ciaran Barr assumed the playmaker role. Serving up ample scoring opportunities for Olcan 'Cloot' McFetridge (who with Donnelly won an All-Star in 1989), Aidan 'Beaver' McCarry and Donal Armstrong, Antrim ran out 4–15 to 1–15 winners. All-Ireland glory beckoned. Dessie remembers,

We were training hard coming up to the All-Ireland final, and to get a bit of a break Paul McKillen and I went to see the All-Ireland football semi-final between Cork and Dublin. As the players were coming on to the field I noticed the big screen for the first time and I said to Paul, 'This should be a great game today.' Paul looked up at the big screen and then he turned around and said to me, 'Is this game live?' I nearly died laughing!

The 1989 All-Ireland semi-final is fondly remembered by all sports fans because of the way the Offaly players made a guard of honour for the Antrim team as they left the pitch.

The Northerners were keen to enjoy their visit to Croke Park for Antrim's first All-Ireland hurling final in forty-six years. They kept pace with Tipperary for the first quarter of the game, creating chances but driving a lot of wides. Then Tipperary got a soft goal which deflated the Northerners. Their play began to drop. Ciaran Barr (the county's first ever All-Star) was very clear why they lost.

We didn't focus properly on the occasion. We were slightly naive and didn't know the pitfalls. Chiefly we were flattered and distracted by too much media attention. The organisation of all our effort fell onto the shoulders of Jim Nelson. A lot of the energies of our backroom team were dissipated, with the result that the players' energies were deflected. It was crazy that the likes of Jim should be worrying about tracksuits and team blazers and shoes, when they should have been focusing on playing matters. Our playing population is so small that there was nobody to come in and take that administrative load off them. In any other county a committee would have rushed into place to help them out.

We found the whole occasion very daunting. We were determined to enjoy the day but we made too many mistakes in the build-up. We arrived far too early and were talking to people so we got caught up in the atmosphere. We were all new to the experience, the management as much as the players. So determined were we to enjoy the experience, we were on the pitch far too early and wasting a lot of energy running around, with the result that physically and emotionally it felt as if we had played half a match. We just couldn't relax.

I was talking to Henry Downey after Derry won the All-Ireland in 1993 and it was interesting to see the contrast between their preparations and ours. They were kept shut off from the media for two weeks and had nothing on their minds only the job that was to be done.

Dessie Donnelly was disappointed by the defeat in the All-Ireland, but thought it was nothing compared to losing to Kilkenny in the All-Ireland semi-final two years later.

That was definitely the biggest low of my career, because we had a couple of opportunities to put Kilkenny away but we didn't take them. A county like us does not get many opportunities to beat a hurling power like Kilkenny, but we blew the chance. It was a make-or-break game for us, and after we lost, the team started to come apart and we never came that close again.

I sometimes compare and contrast our situation with that of Offaly. Both counties have a small hurling base, with only a handful of clubs compared to the big powers. In 1981, in the All-Ireland final against Galway, the gate opened for Offaly late in the game and they ran through it. Offaly hurling reaped the rewards and has been on a roll since. In the Kilkenny match ten years later the gate opened for us, but we stood outside and Antrim hurling went backwards after that.

Of course, there is one important difference between the two counties. Offaly are in the centre not just of Ireland but of the hurling powers. We're tucked up in a corner, 150 miles away from the nearest hurling power.

I remind him that another significant difference between the counties is that Offaly hurling did not have to contend with the Troubles. 'Thankfully the Troubles never had a major impact on me,' he says.

The only time it was an issue for me was when we were travelling for some of the Antrim matches. Of course, you have to be particularly careful when times are especially tense, like the marching season. There are quite a few places in Antrim that you wouldn't walk down the road on your own, or even in company, with a hurley stick in your hand — especially around the Twelfth of July.

Back in the 1970s our changing-rooms were bombed. The damage was superficial. I'd say that was more a matter of luck than careful management on the part of the bombers. There were a lot of theories floating around about who did it, as you can imagine, but I can't tell you who was responsible.

It is said that when men hit mid-life they have to make a big change. Dessie Donnelly responded to this watershed in an unusual way: he became a goalkeeper.

They say you have to be mad to play in goal, so people didn't think it was that strange! I didn't find it that much of a problem, because once you've been used to judging the flight of the ball, it's not as big a change as people might think.

He also doubles up as the club's player-manager. How does he combine the two roles?

It's probably easier be the player-manager when you are goalie than when you play outfield because you see everything that is going on up the field before you. I am lucky that I have good selectors and that helps a lot. Of course, the nice thing is that when I make a mistake the lads are all afraid to criticise me in case they're dropped! I'd like to think so anyway.

He laughs when asked who his most difficult opponent was.

As a forward, it was definitely Kilkenny's Dick O'Hara. I find it very hard to think of the words to describe what it was like to be marked by him — let's just say it was hard to get away from him! As a back, it was Tipperary's Pat Fox. He could do things other forwards couldn't do in their wildest dreams.

He also selected a Kilkenny–Tipperary combination when asked about the greatest players he ever saw.

My number one would have to be Frank Cummins. I marked him in a club match in 1978. Although he was coming to the end of his career at that stage, he still had the 'know-how', and he called the shots and dictated the flow of the game. It was an education just to see him in action. A close second would have to be Nicky English. You sometimes hear a player described as 'a class act'. If there ever was a class act in my time it would have to be Nicky. I also found him to be one of the great characters in the game, though in a quieter way than a lot of players. I would have to say that the best character I ever met was the Down footballer Ambrose Rogers, who died so tragically at the age of thirty-nine in 1999. I got to know him on an All-Stars trip to America and he was great craic.

He considers Ger Loughnane to be the greatest player never to win an All-Ireland medal because of the longevity of his career, his effectiveness as a defender, and his passion for the cause of Clare hurling.

Of the hurlers he competed against, Dessie Donnelly's dream team lines out like this:

Ger Cunningham (Cork)
Sylvie Linnane (Galway) Dick O'Hara (Kilkenny) Dessie Donnelly (Antrim)
Joe Hennessy (Kilkenny) Ger Henderson (Kilkenny) Aidan Fogarty (Offaly)
Frank Cummins (Kilkenny) Michael Coleman (Galway)
Joe Cooney (Galway) John Connolly (Galway) Nicky English (Tipperary)
Liam Fennelly (Kilkenny) Jimmy Barry-Murphy (Cork) Pat Fox (Tipperary)

CAPTAIN FANTASTIC

Hurling-talk is no form of idle gossip in Kilkenny, but a crucial element in the county's psyche. Business, love and the land regularly take second place to the fortunes of local teams, as the great Dublin football team of the 1970s found when they visited the Marble City for a league fixture. They were gratified to see a huge crowd at the ground, but when the mighty Heffo's army took the field their pride was severely dented: the majority of the crowd had gone home after the warm-up game, a minors' hurling championship fixture among local clubs.

Joe Dunphy has the rare distinction in Kilkenny hurling of captaining his native county to two consecutive All-Ireland minor titles, in 1961 and 1962. A study in self-effacement, his face purples with embarrassment when he is queried about his appointment.

The captain really had to be from Mooncoin because we

Joe Dunphy is presented with the 1961 All-Ireland Minor trophy.

had won four minor county titles. Three of us minors were selected for the senior team, so it was between us. Our driver, the late Richard Croke, sorted it out by getting us to draw straws.

'It was a great honour to be captain,' he says, 'though I had very shaky legs!'

Winning his first All-Ireland brought home to Dunphy the importance of hurling in Kilkenny.

After we won the All-Ireland minor final there was a bonfire in the town of Mooncoin in our honour. After all the fuss had died down I went back to my home place, Luffany, a little village with just fourteen farmhouses. There was a field at the back of the house where as young fellas we had always trained and practised, supervised by a man called Bob Collins, who would be timing us as we made runs around the field and so on. Bob hardly ever left the village. That night when I got back from Mooncoin, there was Bob in the field with a bonfire blazing for me. It brought tears to my eyes.

Dunphy made his senior debut for Kilkenny in a league fixture in 1964 but he was unable to hold down a regular place until Mooncoin's victory in the county final in 1965 proved to be the catalyst for his breakthrough onto the senior team. How intimidating was it to walk into a dressing-room which held some of the greatest hurlers of all time?

You walked in, togged out and kept your head down! Having said that, even the most established stars were very supportive. Eddie Keher, in particular, was very friendly. He would always talk to you before a game, give you a few words of encouragement and try to help you relax. I remember well him taking a couple of us new lads for a walk down O'Connell Street the evening before a big match. I had a few other walks with him too.

Although Dunphy won a National League medal the game's highest honour eluded him.

In 1966 Kilkenny lost the All-Ireland to Cork, 3-9 to 1-10, although we were red-hot favourites. I scored a point, but it wasn't a happy memory for me because I had missed a goal a couple of minutes earlier.

The papers the next day were full of talk about 'the year of the sleeping pill'. It was the first year players had taken them before an All-Ireland final. There was a lot of smart comments afterwards that we took them too late, because we hadn't fully woke up until after the match.

What was the highlight of his career?

I would say there were three highlights: winning the two minor All-Irelands, winning the National League, and winning the county championship in 1965 with Mooncoin. I'd say that was the biggest honour of my life, because we had never won it before and we've never won it since.

He considers Christy Ring the greatest hurler he ever saw, and lists off a string of Kilkenny players as amongst the best in the game. He has a particular admiration for Eddie Keher, for his skill, dedication and attention to detail.

Perfectionists like Keher get the little things right. Dunphy recalls a famous incident from the 1974 Leinster hurling final. With the sides tied and only seconds to go, the legendary corner-forward was fouled and Kilkenny were awarded a free. The lace on Keher's boot was broken in the tackle, and he knew he would not be able to score unless the lace was tied, so he bent down and tied it. The Wexford fans thought he was engaged in gamesmanship and let him know with a chorus of booing. Keher, however, kept his concentration and slotted the sliotar between the posts to win the match.

Given his passion for the black and amber, it's not surprising Joe Dunphy thinks the Kilkenny team of the early 1970s was the greatest team of all time. He is not alone in this view, a fact I discovered when I posed the same question to Gaelic games commentator Mícheál Ó Muircheartaigh.

I think that hurling has changed a lot for the better, and many of the players — and this has amazed me, because generally a lot of players hang on to the theory that their own generation was the best — that hurled maybe thirty years ago are admitting that the modern generation of hurlers are better than they were. I think that video evidence would swing you around to that view. There is a greater emphasis on skill now. In the past, the man was played more. Now, it was never as bad as football, but there was a lot of holding in the old days. For example, full-backs penned into the forwards, they held on to their man when the ball came in and kept their man away from the goalie. That would all be deemed a foul nowadays. The emphasis now is on speed and skill, and I think hurling is the better for that.

When you talk about the great teams, it's not near as clear-cut in hurling as it is in football. If I were pushed to it, I would say that the best hurling team — with the emphasis on team — that I ever saw was the Kilkenny team of the early 1970s. They won the All-Ireland in 1972, 1974 and 1975 and played the final in 1973 against Limerick. I think of their great games, especially against Wexford, who had a great team at the time but could not get the better of Kilkenny. I think that Kilkenny team was good in all sectors: take Eddie Keher in the full-forward line, Pat Delaney at centre-forward, Frank Cummins in midfield, Pat Henderson at centre half-back. They had supermen in all parts of the field and played like a team.

I suppose I'd have to single out Eddie Keher from that team as one of the all-time greats. I always say that to score a point in an All-Ireland final is something special for a player, and I think it's seven goals and seventy-seven points that he scored in All-Ireland finals alone. That tally is a measure of the man's greatness.

D.J. Carey is the modern star, there is no doubt about it. The crowd get very excited when the ball comes towards him. He has speed and tremendous skill. On his day he is unbeatable, and maybe the best of him hasn't been seen yet.

I always say that you have to wait a few years after a guy retires to judge him properly. Eddie Keher played senior for Kilkenny for the first time in 1959, having starred in the minor All-Ireland final that year. The senior final ended in a draw and he was drafted on as a sub for the replay. He was still playing for the seniors in 1977. Apart from his superb skill, the fact that he remained at the top for so long is also a factor.

Dunphy is proud of Kilkenny's tradition of sportsmanship. He tells a story from the 1958 All-Ireland semi-final between Tipperary and Kilkenny to illustrate this. When Tipperary's Jimmy Doyle scored eight points off Paddy Buggy, a Kilkenny

supporter asked Paddy after the match, 'What happened? Why
didn't you hit him?'

'Why should I?' Buggy replied. 'He didn't hit me.'

Kilkenny hurling has sired many characters and Joe Dunphy
has seen plenty of them.

*Paddy Grace was very likeable and would never let you down if you
were looking for tickets. The only time he did was after we won the
minor All-Ireland in 1961. All of us went to him and asked if he
would get us tickets for the All-Ireland football final between Offaly
and Down. He told us to meet him outside Barry's Hotel before the
match, but as it turned out the final attracted a record crowd and
when we met him he had no tickets for us. We got into the match by
climbing over the Railway Wall and paying ten pence for the
privilege.*

*Our 'bag-carrier' for the two minor All-Irelands, 'Thew' Leahy,
was a great character. He carried me off the field after we won both
finals. Ollie Walsh was also a wonderful character. At the railway
station after we lost the All-Ireland in 1966, Ollie got on board the
luggage car and started driving it around the platform. It's a wonder
he wasn't arrested!*

Dunphy speaks of Ollie Walsh with such high regard it comes
as no surprise that Ollie was an automatic choice on his dream
team. The side in full is:

Ollie Walsh (Kilkenny)
John Doyle (Tipperary) Nick O'Donnell (Wexford) Denis Murphy (Cork)
Seamie Cleere (Kilkenny) Pat Henderson (Kilkenny) Sean McMahon (Clare)
Mick Roche (Tipperary) Martin Coogan (Kilkenny)
Jimmy Doyle (Tipperary) Christy Ring (Cork) Eddie Keher (Kilkenny)
D.J. Carey (Kilkenny) Nicky Rackard (Wexford) Tom Walsh (Kilkenny)

HURLING IN THE CONGO

Waterford's sole representative on the Team of the Century is right full-back Jim Fives. He first made his name as a forward with Waterford and his club, Tourin. Jim was the youngest of five brothers who all played senior hurling with their native county, and the family also played a prominent role in their local club's development. A student at Lismore CBS, which had a strong team in the 1930s, Jim played for Waterford minors in 1947, but was over age the following year when they went on to win the All-Ireland. The Waterford players who won the All-Ireland hurling title in 1948 were his heroes, particularly centre half-back John Keane. His ambition was to play for his county, and with his substantial physical presence, the six-foot-tall Jim Fives was always likely to play at senior level.

Hurling was a hard code.

In 1948 I played a senior club match in Waterford. It was a very niggly game and there was a lot of moaning to the referee, the great Limerick player, Garrett Howard. At half-time he brought the two teams together and said, 'Let's have no more of this whinging. Hurling is a man's game. It's not tennis. Be men and take your challenges and your punishment. Go back out there and play like men, not mice.' We took his advice to heart and went out and played like men possessed. Nobody held back. There were some fierce challenges, and an awful lot of sore limbs the next day!

In 1949 he entered the Irish Army as a cadet in the Curragh, County Kildare, and played hurling with the army team, which brought him up against inter-county hurlers such as Mossy Riordan of Cork, Dublin's Liam Donnelly, and Billy O'Neill, who played for Cork and Galway. He also made his debut for Waterford against Wexford. It was a baptism of fire as his immediate opponent was no less a player than Billy Rackard. Waterford's defeat that day was to be an omen of things to come.

The biggest disappointment of my time with Waterford came when we lost to Tipperary by two points in the Munster championship in 1951. They were the big power then, and we were so close. We never put it together after that.

Why did Waterford have so little success?

The Waterford team that won the All-Ireland in 1948 was a relatively old team and they broke up straight after that win. We had a poor team while I was there. You have to remember that it's a small county and the number of clubs playing the game is small. Another problem was that we had not the right management structures. We had far too

Jim Fives and his army colleagues pose before the Galway Hurling Final, 1955. Back (L–R): Lt B. O'Neill, Cpl P. Ryan, Lt F. Stewart, Sgt R. Quinn, Lt T. Leyne, Pte T. Crowley, Lt J. Young, Lt N. Sheridan, Lt J. Kissane, Sgt A. Flannery. Front (L–R): S. Aherne, Pte P. Barry, Pte G. Deering, Lt J. Fives, Sgt J. Brophy, Pte J. Bowen, Lt S. Murphy, Pte J. Mernagh.

many selectors and this led to a lot of 'political' selection decisions, with selectors sometimes more interested in having players from their club on the team than having the fifteen best players. Of course, that was not a problem unique to Waterford, but at the time we couldn't afford to be going out with a weaker side.

After cadet school Fives was transferred to Renmore in Galway, and for the next four years he continued to play for Waterford even though he was playing his club football and hurling in the west. He played at midfield with the army, on a team which boasted inter-county players like Jimmy Brophy from Kilkenny and Dublin's Joe Young, and won a Galway county championship medal.

It was a very quiet time in Irish history to be a soldier. Ireland had not yet begun its peacekeeping missions overseas, which meant that we had plenty of time for sport.

He played for two years with the Waterford senior football team, but the closest he got to winning a county hurling medal came in 1955, when they lost the county final. Afterwards, Fives made the difficult decision to forsake his beloved county and declare for Galway.

It wasn't near as easy then to move around from Galway to Waterford as it is now. I was also often caught between the club and county. The club sometimes wanted me for a big match when Waterford would want me on the same day for a league match or a tournament game. Really, for practical reasons the only option for me was to switch to Galway, although I was very sorry not to be playing for Waterford any more.

The hardest part was when I had to play for Galway against Waterford — in the All-Ireland semi-final in 1957 and in 1959. We played them in the Munster championship because Galway were 'in Munster' then. It's a very, very difficult thing to play against your native county.

As had been the case with Waterford, Fives played for Galway during lean times. The highlight was winning the Oireachtas final by a big score over Wexford in 1958. They also enjoyed some good performances in the Railway Cup, notably a draw with Munster in 1957 and a victory over Leinster in the 1959 semi-final, but Munster beat them in the final in the newly renovated Croke Park.

Fives's move to Galway coincided with a switch from playing in the forwards to the backs.

I was anxious to play in the backs because I always like to be facing the ball. The thing about forward play is that you always have to turn once you get possession.

A serious back injury caused him to step down from senior inter-county hurling in 1959, but two years later he was transferred to Castlerea and came out of retirement to play junior hurling for Roscommon. In 1964 Fives was transferred once more, and had hardly arrived at his new posting in Castlebar when he was asked if he would play for Mayo the following Sunday. The old back injury had returned, however, and Fives was forced to decline the offer. He had already played football for one county and hurling for three others.

While medals were few and far between, Jim Fives won many representative honours. In 1953 he played for Ireland against the Universities, and the following year, when the Universities were not thought strong enough to field a testing opposition, Fives was chosen on the Combined Services team — made up of players from the universities, the gardaí and the army — to play Ireland. In 1959 he captained the Rest of Ireland in a prestige fixture against All-Ireland champions Tipperary.

When the Irish Army began its UN peacekeeping duties, Fives served on two missions, spending six months in the Congo and six months in the Middle East. 'It was very interesting, but very tense and demanding,' he recalls. The soldiers played hurling during their free time. 'The kindest thing I can say about our pitches,' Fives remarks, 'is that they were very dusty!'

He has no difficulty deciding on the greatest player he ever saw.

I never saw Mick Mackey play, so it has to be Christy Ring. I marked him in Railway Cup matches. It was a very trying experience as a back because, not alone did you never know what he was going to do, a lot of the time you never knew where he was! He just ghosted into positions. One minute you were right beside him — the next he was gone and you were left for dead.

He has enduring respect for many former opponents.

As a forward my most difficult opponent was 'Diamond' Hayden, and as a back the most difficult were Sean Clohessy, Tim Flood and Liam Deavaney. I always felt that Liam was a very under-rated player. He was also a very clean player.

He laughs heartily when asked about his favourite character in the game.

It has to be Kilkenny's 'Diamond' Hayden. At the time there wasn't as much contact between players from the different counties as there is now, but in 1951 we went with Kilkenny to London, so I got to know Diamond then. He was a great believer in psychological warfare. He would do everything and anything to put you off your game. He was always talking himself up, always trying to get you to think that you would be much better off trying to find someone else to mark.

I believe Christy Ring played those sort of mind games as well, though he never did on me. He probably felt that he didn't need to.

Fives has seen great changes in hurling since his retirement.

The game is very fast now, which is a great thing. However, I'm disappointed that there is so little emphasis on ground hurling and also that there is very little overhead hurling. It's almost as if catching the ball has become everything. I also think too much allowance is made for the player who is in possession, especially the way they are allowed take too many steps.

Now retired from the army, Fives is immersed in voluntary work with the Irish Heart Foundation, and keeps himself in shape with a lot of exercise and golf. Nobody enjoyed Waterford's 1998 revival more than Fives.

It was wonderful to see, and I hope Waterford hurling fans will not have to wait as long again to see their county up there with the big powers in hurling.

Fives began his dream team selection with Tony Reddin, the legendary Tipperary goalkeeper who became part of hurling folklore after an altercation with Cork player and politician, Jack Lynch. During the white heat of a Cork versus Tipp clash, Lynch charged into Reddin and in the process bundled both of them into the net. Reddin had something of a speech impediment, but still managed to roar: 'F-f-f-fuck you, Lynch. Try that again an' there'll be a f-f-f-fuckin' by-election.'

Fives's ideal side from the players of his era is:

Tony Reddin (Tipperary)
Bobby Rackard (Wexford) Nick O'Donnell (Wexford) Jimmy Brohan (Cork)
Seamie Cleere (Kilkenny) John Keane (Waterford) Iggy Clarke (Galway)
Jackie Salmon (Galway) Jack Lynch (Cork)
Josie Gallagher (Galway) Mick Mackey (Limerick) Christy Ring (Cork)
Paddy Kenny (Tipperary) Nick Rackard (Wexford) Jimmy Smyth (Clare)

LICENCE TO THRILL

Limerick's sole representative on the Team of the Century, drawn from players who never won an All-Ireland medal, was the late Sean Herbert. In his twelve-year career with Limerick, the Ahane man played in five Munster finals without winning any of them. The closest he came to it was in 1944, when Limerick drew with Cork. In the replay, the Shannonsiders were leading by five points with fifteen minutes to go, but Cork pegged back the lead to draw level. Then in the dying seconds the wizard of Cloyne struck. Never were truer words spoken:

> *Now Cork is bate,*
> *the hay is saved,*
> *the thousands wildly sing –*
> *They speak too soon,*
> *my sweet garsún,*
> *'cos here comes Christy Ring.*

Ring got the sliotar and made a forty-yard solo run which has become part of hurling legend, before unleashing a powerful shot for the decisive goal. After the match Ring's brother, Willie John, asked him why he had not gone for safety and taken a point. 'Anyone could have scored a point!' Ring replied.

In 1984, the same year as Sean Herbert was being selected on the Team of the Century, Gary Kirby was coming to prominence winning an All-Ireland minor medal with Limerick and taking his first senior county medal with Patrickswell. Three years later he helped Limerick to an All-Ireland under-21 title and captained the

Irish under-21 shinty team, and in 1986 he made his senior debut for Limerick. But the honours came less quickly at county level than they did with Patrickswell.

We won the Munster club title in 1988, but it was even sweeter to win it again two years later, when we beat Éire Óg of Ennis by 0–8 to 0–6. We were without Ciaran Carey because he had been suspended in controversial circumstances, and that bothered us. We also finished the game with only fourteen men, so that made it one of our proudest days.

Glenmore deprived Patrickswell of the All-Ireland club title in 1991, but Kirby at least had the consolation of winning the first of his four All-Star awards that year.

Limerick's David Hanly, writing in *Ireland of the Welcomes,* observed perceptively:

Any definition of Irish culture which excludes the Munster hurling final would be, to put it mildly, inadequate. Yet it is doubtful if the majority of self-consciously cultured people would spontaneously pronounce the final a central and important part of Irish culture, their idea of culture being cripplingly circumscribed by a dictionary definition: culture ... the intellectual side of civilisation. There is nothing even vaguely intellectual about a Munster hurling final, yet a proper enjoyment of the game presupposes a sophisticated appreciation of the finer things.

Gary Kirby reached the heights of hurling culture, and the high point of his career, at a Munster final in 1994.

My greatest and fondest memory would have to be looking down on the Thurles field, seeing it full with Limerick people waving their green and white, and as captain lifting the Munster Cup after we beat Clare.

Gary Kirby takes on a bloody-nosed opponent.

The All-Ireland hurling final that autumn was one of the most dramatic matches in the history of the game. Limerick outplayed Offaly throughout the match and with just minutes remaining held an apparently unassailable five-points lead. Then Offaly's Johnny Dooley scored a goal from a free. Within a minute, Pat O'Connor had a second goal. Limerick floundered, while Offaly's players suddenly looked as if they could score points at will. A new joke was born. Why are Limerick magic? Because they can disappear for five minutes.

Kirby had won a National League medal in 1992, when Limerick made a dramatic comeback against Tipperary to snatch a one-point victory in injury time. What was it like to be on the opposite end of the experience?

> *It's a feeling I wouldn't wish on anyone. With seven minutes to go, I felt I would be going up to be presented with the Liam McCarthy Cup. Then, all of a sudden, it was gone. Something happened in the last five minutes. You can't analyse it. It was a huge disappointment.*

One of the complications of the fixture was that Offaly were managed by a legend of Limerick hurling, Eamonn Cregan. Offaly's Joe Dooley thought:

> *It was a very awkward position for Eamonn, having hurled for so long with Limerick himself and because he lived down there, but it didn't affect his preparations for Offaly. He didn't use his in-depth knowledge of the Limerick players much. He never spoke about the strengths and weaknesses of particular Limerick players unless we asked him about them.*
>
> *I can't remember anything Eamonn said to us before the final, but I recall very vividly his team-talk at half-time. I can assure you it was unprintable! He was very worked up. None of us dared to speak, except briefly among ourselves.*

Two years later, Limerick were back in the Munster final after snatching victory from All-Ireland champions, Clare, in the final minutes of the semi-final. Limerick went all the way to the All-Ireland final again that year, but it was to be Liam Griffin's

Wexford that claimed the title. The match itself was a personal disappointment for Kirby.

I got a broken finger in the first five minutes. I remember going over towards the Cusack Stand to take a free from near midfield. I was trying to stop the bleeding before I took it, but as I took the free I felt a searing pain go up my hand.

There was a controversy after the match about the manner in which the Limerick team broke prematurely from the parade, but Kirby feels the incident does not merit much comment.

The reason we broke was that throughout the year we broke at the same time, but no one told us before the match that we had to go around the full distance. In 1994 I was told not to break, but in 1996 no one said anything to Ciaran Carey, so how was he to know? There was no reason behind it — for us, it was just normal to break at that point.

Limerick has been on the threshold of hurling honours for many years, but why has the county not gone all the way?

It's hard to say why Limerick haven't won an All-Ireland in my time. One of the main reasons is that we have being unlucky. We played in two finals, and against Offaly it was just one of those things. In the Wexford game I felt a few vital decisions went against us, especially the goal we had disallowed.

Kirby is one of the most prolific scorers in the game. Is there any score which is etched in his memory?

Every score is important, whether it is your first one or your last one. I scored a few important ones for the club. I suppose for the county, the 2-4 I got against Cork in the 1994 championship had a big impact as it set us off on a great year.

Gary Kirby has played under a number of high-profile managers, all of them with different styles.

Tom Ryan had a strong presence about him and knew what he wanted. He related that to the players and everyone knew where they stood. Eamonn Cregan is a different type, who gets more involved in the training of the team. He got players trying to play a more open type of game. While they are great managers, the one I really enjoyed was Phil Bennis. Phil coached both our minor and under-21 sides that won the All-Ireland. He also trains our club, Patrickswell, and seems to understand every player individually and what his strengths are. He has a great understanding with the players.

'Everyone involved in the GAA adds something to the game,' Kirby continues, 'as each person has a different character.'

Some don't say much but just get on with it, others just can't stop talking, while others are great at ball-hopping and bringing laughter to the dressing-room. When we won the minor and under-21 All-Irelands our goalie, Val Murnane, was one of those who always brought a relaxed atmosphere to the dressing-room. Mike Houlihan is another great character. He always had a strong presence about him, one you would always want with you.

Selecting his dream team was difficult, particularly because he had to exclude players like Brian Whelahan, Brian Corcoran and Leonard Enright. His team is:

Tommy Quaid (Limerick)
Sylvie Linnane (Galway) Brian Lohan (Clare) Martin Hanamy (Offaly)
Peter Finnerty (Galway) Ger Henderson (Kilkenny) Tom Cashman (Cork)
Frank Cummins (Kilkenny) John Fenton (Cork)
D.J. Carey (Kilkenny) Joe Cooney (Galway) Nicky English (Tipperary)
Jimmy Barry-Murphy (Cork) Ray Cummins (Cork) Eamonn Cregan (Limerick)

THE STAR OF THE COUNTY DOWN

Máirín McAleenan made her senior debut for the Down camogie team in March 1986. It was a coming of age for the wing-forward, who would go on to win almost all of camogie's honours. She won the Down Senior Camogie Championships and Senior League, the Ulster Club Championships — senior, minor and junior — as well as the Ulster Minor League. She also won the All-Ireland Junior Championship, All-Ireland Junior National League and All-Ireland Intermediate Championship. She has been Ulster GAA Writers Player of the Year, and Player of the Tournament at both the Kilmacud Sevens and the Ashbourne Cup.

McAleenan has collected most of the game's trophies, except an All-Ireland title.

Camogie exploded into her life at an early age.

Maureen McAleenan with her mother, Mary, after Liatroim Fontenoy's win in the 1998 Ulster Club Championship.

My earliest memory of camogie is torturing my brother, John, to make me a stick so that I could join in the five-a-side matches which my eight brothers and sister, Brid, played every evening on our front street. Having just turned five, I had come of age, you see, and although my brother Ciarán was just a tachrán — *only three years old — he got the call-up too on the very same evening. I consoled myself with the fact that he was there only to make up the numbers.*

I was duly measured up and such important details as distance from the ground to my hinchbone were noted. After what seemed like a lifetime, I was finally presented with a plank of wood about a foot-and-a-half in length. It narrowed abruptly at one end, and this, I was told, was the handle. I got splinters in both hands from the hours I spent practising with it after school and long into the darkness.

I progressed to striking stray balls to the hurlers at their training sessions, and at around eight years of age I started training with Liatroim Fontenoys. Since then I have been very proud to be 'a Liatroim Fontenoy'.

Her years with the club have left Máirín McAleenan with a host of fond memories — of inter-county star Sheila McCartan presenting her with her very own Liatroim senior camogie jersey, of winning Féile na nGael Division 3 in Wexford in 1984, and 'almost bursting with pride' at the brilliant Liatroim performance in the Ulster Club Championship final in 1998.

My biggest disappointments were losing the Down Championship final in 1990; the poor performance of the Down team in the All-Ireland intermediate final against Limerick in 1996; the poor performance of Liatroim Fontenoys in the Ulster Club Championship final against Loughguile in 1997; and not being selected on Liatroim Fontenoys team for the Down final in 1989.

Her ambition is of course to win an All-Ireland senior medal, but as a primary-school teacher she is particularly concerned also that the future generation of camogie players, part of the largest female sporting organisation in Ireland, with some 80,000 members, be adequately nurtured. She gives an upbeat forecast of the status of the game in the years ahead.

In the year 2004 I would envisage fifteen-a-side camogie as a well-marketed sport gaining in popularity, regularly played in conjunction with major GAA games, which would heighten its profile even more. By the time the Association's centenary is upon us, I would expect it to be moving towards the purchase of its own central ground in each county. The appointment of full-time camogie coaches at schools level in all counties would also be anticipated, as would the organisation of Comórtas na nGaelscoileanna, which would grow together with an Ghaeilge at primary school level. It would be pleasing to see camogie being played widely at school and underage level.

What advice would she give to young players?

Many people would advise players to practise the skills until you can do them right. I would say, though, that you should practise them until you can't do them wrong. Secondly, listen to your coaches — give them and other players respect. Respect referees, too, for whatever decisions they make. Although you may not agree with it, they, like the players, do their best. Thirdly, play every game as if it were your last, and aim to enjoy it as if it were your first. You must always play with dedication, determination and discipline.

To what does she attribute her own success as a player?

Any achievements which I have attained in camogie come as a result of the hard work of all team members. I think it is unfair, in a team game, that scoring forwards always grab the headlines, while defenders and midfielders are rarely recognised for their contribution.

Máirín has played with great players at club, county and provincial level. She recalls how Down's Bonnie McGreevy 'talked incessantly throughout a match', and instilled confidence in her team-mates with her ability to score. 'She scored an unforgettable goal against Tipperary in the All-Ireland junior final in 1991.' Club-mate Donna Greeran was never less than totally committed: 'Donna would rather be chased by a rotweiler than give away a score!'

Another clubmate is Bernie Kelly, who at forty-three continues to power Liatroim's efforts from midfield, twenty-two years after helping her club to their first Down senior title. Proof of her endurance shows:

She scored a goal in each of the All-Ireland junior finals of 1976 and 1991, and picked up the Player of the Tournament in the Ulster club seven-a-side competition in 1999.

Máirín recalls,

On the way to the Ulster club final in 1998, I was reading a newspaper article on the match, and the journalist had put Bernie in the 'veteran' bracket and questioned the wisdom of playing her in midfield at such a high level of camogie. 'Do you hear that, Bernie,' I said to her, 'they reckon here that you're past it!'

'Huh! Past it!' said Bernie, 'I'll be hurling for Liatroim when I'm fucking ninety!'

Foremost among Máirín's heroines are Angela and Ann Downey of Kilkenny, who made a fantastic contribution to camogie in the 1980s and 1990s.

Their longevity at the highest level is amazing, and I believe will never be equalled, not to mention surpassed. Ann is fiery, strong, tough and a non-stop runner. Angela was like lightning and skilful beyond belief. Camogie owes a great deal to the Downeys.

Off the field there were great characters, like Down's Theresa Allen, Claire McGrath and Joan Henderson, 'hilariously entertaining during training sessions and on the way to and from matches.'
Asked about her most difficult opponent, Máirín's answer is less than straightforward.

It's very difficult to say who my toughest opponent was, since it depended on my own form and that of my opponents — which could fluctuate greatly. For example, I can recall scoring two or three goals and four or five points while marking Cork captain Eithne Duggan in a Gael Linn final a couple of years ago. However, the next evening I only managed a couple of points in a Down league match, while marking a player who wouldn't be considered county material.

One of the toughest opponents would be Deirdre Costello, Galway minor centre half-back, in the All-Ireland semi-final in 1985. I remember wondering how a sixteen-year-old could be so physically strong. Ann Lenihan, Limerick, is a very tight marker and frustrates a forward with her hooking, blocking, hassling, and nudging the sliotar just beyond the forward's reach. Catherine Murphy, Rathnure, inspires confidence with her excellent reading of the game, and her lengthy clearances; she is a very experienced defender.

Given the difficulties McAleenan experienced choosing her most difficult opponent, it is not surprising that choosing her dream team posed problems as well.

The difficulty in picking a team is that, since Down was absent from senior championship camogie for over a decade, I have had little opportunity to play against many of the country's top players on a regular basis, apart from third-level education, club championship and inter-provincial competition. I would argue that it would have been a lot easier for me to select a hurling dream team, since hurling enjoys a much higher media profile and the public has the chance to watch league, championship, club championship and university competitions regularly.

The players I have selected are players I have played with or against, and who in my opinion have extra-special qualities. Many, many excellent players have been left out of my final fifteen — like Sandy Fitzgibbon and Irene O'Keeffe (Cork); Triona Bonnar and Sinéad Nealon (Tipperary); Denise O'Boyle and Bróna McCorry (Antrim); Ann Reddy and Ger Codd (Wexford) and Germaine Noonan (Dublin).

Others, who I feel are excellent but have not been playing long enough at the height of their career to be considered, include Veronica Curtin, Denise Gilligan and Therese Maher (Galway), Eileen O'Brien and Vera Sheehan (Limerick) and Jane Adams (Antrim).'

Máirín McAleenan's dream team is as follows:

Louise Curry (Galway)
Donna Greeran (Down) Catherine Murphy (Wexford) Pamela Nevin (Galway)
Denise Cronin (Cork) Sarah-Annie Quinn (Derry) Moira McMahon (Clare)
Sharon Glynn (Galway) Linda Mellerick (Cork)
Sinéad Millea (Kilkenny) Lynn Dunlea (Cork) Fiona O'Driscoll (Cork)
Angela Downey (Kilkenny) Deirdre Hughes (Tipperary) Grace McMullan (Antrim)

THE PURPLE AND GOLD

Martin Quigley made his senior debut for Wexford in 1970 and became part of a unique piece of family history in that year's All-Ireland final when he played with his brothers, Pat and John, to create an all-Quigley half-forward line for the county, while another brother, 'Big Dan', was selected at centre-back. An injury-stricken Wexford amassed a highly creditable 5–10 that day, but Cork ran up a massive 6–21 to take the All-Ireland title.

Quigley played his last game for his county nineteen years later. In the course of his career he won four consecutive All-Stars, from 1973–76, and was chosen at centre half-forward on the centenary team of the greatest players never to have won an All-Ireland.

He was born into a hurling mixed-marriage: his mother had virtually no interest in the game while his father was fanatical in his devotion. 'I remember as a kid going to a lot of matches with him. That's where we got our enthusiasm from. Once, he invited a referee to the line for a fight. In his later years he had to give up going to matches. He used to get totally worked up, which wasn't very good for him.

My earliest hurling memory goes back to 1960, when I was nine years of age, listening to the great Mícheál O'Hehir commentating on the All-Ireland hurling final when Wexford beat Tipperary. After the match was over I went out in the fields to bring in the cows, armed with my hurl and ball and pretending to be both Billy Rackard and Tim Flood.

I was fourteen when I was brought to my first All-Ireland in 1965. Nowadays children are taken to Croke Park at the age of seven or eight, but when you are not going to big matches the media is so important, and Mícheál was the best evangelist hurling could ever have. I think his commentaries had an unmerciful bearing on my development as a player.

I'm glad that we have had so much hurling on television in recent years. There were people who said attendances would drop once matches were televised, but the opposite has happened, because television has whetted people's appetite for the game.

My love of hurling really took off when I went to St Peter's College. We won a lot of colleges' titles at juvenile, junior and senior levels. The highlights were winning the All-Ireland colleges' titles in 1967 and '68, both after replays. I played for three years for the county minor team from 1967–69, and we beat Cork to win the minor All-Ireland in 1968.

Wexford had an assembly line of new talent coming through in the 1950s and '60s. The production line slowed considerably in the 1970s, however, and Martin Quigley was one of the victims of this change in Wexford's fortunes.

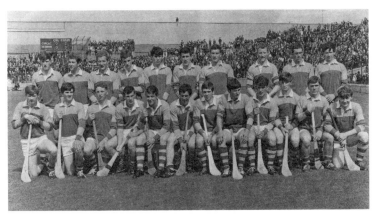

Wexford prepare to battle against Cork. Back (L–R): *James Murphy, Pat Cox, Paddy Breen, Aidan Carrigan, Jack Russell, Paddy O'Connor, Tom Byrne, Thomas Walsh, Kenny Welsh, Denis Kinsella.*
Front (L–R): *Martin Quigley, Larry Doyle, Mick Butler, Martin Casey, George O'Connor, Larry Kinsella, Martin Byrne, Phil Kennedy, Larry Byrne, Peter O'Brien, Liam Bennett, Matt Wickham*

When I ask him about the greatest moment of his career, he answers immediately: 'Our Leinster Final win of 1976. Kilkenny had beaten us in the previous five finals, but we beat them by seventeen points that year. I remember looking at the clock with about ten minutes to go and we were leading by fifteen or sixteen points, and I thought to myself, there's nothing they can do to us now, though with Kilkenny you can never know.

It was such an unusual feeling for me to be so confident against them, that's why I remember the incident so well. The game went reasonably well for me, though nothing exceptional. It was one day when it was all about the team.

As happens so often in sport, that year also saw his greatest disappointment.

We really should have won the All-Ireland that year, having been eight points up against Cork after ten minutes. We had really good teams in Wexford in the seventies and we were very unfortunate not to have won at least one All-Ireland in those years.

One of his best displays for Wexford was in a league fixture against Clare at Tulla, 'a graveyard for visiting teams', which earned him the accolade Sportstar of the Week. Apart from his pride in wearing the purple and gold, Quigley also drew great enjoyment from wearing the black and amber of Rathnure.

I was part of a very strong Rathnure team and I have ten senior championship medals. For the bulk of my club career I played as I did for Wexford, in the forwards. In the later stages I switched to full-back, and had many a mighty tussle with the legendary Tony Doran.

'The approach to the game in Rathnure was purist,' he recalls. 'The support within the parish was fantastic.' The Quigley family was the backbone of the Rathnure side that reached the All-Ireland club final in 1972 and '74, only to lose on both occasions to Blackrock.

By the mid-1980s, Quigley was forced to consider where his career in hurling was going. 'I'm not sure did I retire or was I retired in 1986,' he says wryly, adding:

There are some who would say I had a more spectacular comeback than Lazarus. In 1988 I was a spectator at the first round championship game against Laois. Three weeks later I scored 2–2 against Kilkenny.

Quigley wears the scars of a long career. He remembers one escapade:

In a league match against Offaly I was hit on the back of my head as I went for a dropping ball. At half-time our mentors examined it and I had nine stitches inserted without any anaesthetic. I just clinched my teeth and braced myself. When the question was raised if I was fit to continue, it was said, 'He's a hardy young fellow and he'll be all right.' Out I went for the second half, when it was the last place I should have gone.

How would he like to be remembered as a player by Wexford fans? 'As a whole-hearted player who always gave his best.'

He retired in 1989, but soon found he 'missed the buzz of hurling'. A new role beckoned when he was asked to pilot the Wexford team's fortunes. He could not refuse, though the job was no bed of roses.

Managing is not nearly as enjoyable as playing. When you are playing you only have to worry about your own job, but when you're the manager you have to worry about everybody else. There are so many things outside your control, from players getting injured to bad referees' decisions which can cost you a game.

When I retired as a player, I got involved in managing Wexford almost immediately. With the benefit of hindsight, I should have taken a break from the game and turned to management later, but while hindsight is great it's not any good when you have to make a decision. I should have given myself a bit of distance before making the switch from playing to managing. It's hard to have a clear perspective when emotionally you're too close to the centre of things.

How would he assess his own term in charge of Wexford?

I'm not the best person to judge. Ultimately, a manager is judged by results. In my three years in charge we got to two National League finals, but we won nothing. I suppose, though, any manager is only as good as the players he has at his disposal.

This may well have been the reason that Babs Keating once remarked about management, 'It's a very short distance between a slap on the back and a kick in the arse!'

In 1991 Quigley stepped down as trainer, and now confines himself to coaching under-age teams with his son's club, St Martin's. Wexford's new manager, Christy Keogh, enlisted the services of Cyril Farrell to prepare the team for the Leinster championship, particularly the inevitable clash with old rivals Kilkenny. The move did not have the desired impact, however, as Kilkenny inflicted a heavy defeat on the Slaneysiders. What does Quigley think of the comment that, instead of rallying Wexford, Farrell's presence helped inspire Kilkenny?

I wouldn't pay any heed to that sort of talk. Anyone who thinks that Kilkenny need Cyril Farrell's involvement to be fully motivated to beat Wexford in the championship knows nothing about hurling, and Kilkenny hurling in particular. Kilkenny had a strong team that year and beat us badly. I don't think it would have made much difference who was managing us that particular year. The one thing that Cyril's involvement did achieve was to dramatically heighten expectations within the county. Not for the first time, though, they were to be cruelly dashed.

In 1996, however, Wexford became the home of hurling, All-Ireland glory a story of paradise regained. Why did they win the All-Ireland that year and not earlier?

The key match in 1996 was not the All-Ireland final, but beating Offaly in the Leinster final. That set them up as a team of winners. And the supporters played a huge part in Wexford's win, almost as much as the team itself. It was fascinating to see the way support snowballed throughout the championship. It was said there were 8,000 Wexford fans at the Kilkenny match, but there were 40,000 there for the final.

I think there were two crucial factors which explain why Wexford won that year. Firstly, there was manager Liam Griffin and the passion, motivation, organisation and leadership he gave to the team. Secondly, there was Damien Fitzhenry. He's the best goalie in Ireland, in my opinion. If I had to pinpoint one player on the pitch who meant the difference between victory and defeat in 1996, it would be him.

When Liam Griffin quit as county manager in 1999, the media speculated that Quigley might be tempted to take on the job again. He dismissed the suggestion immediately.

No way. I don't think people appreciate the sacrifices that are involved or the time commitment that is required. I don't want to offend teachers, but maybe if I had a lot of free time like them I might be interested, but not when I am self-employed [he has an accountancy practice]. *The pressures are getting stronger all the time, partly because of the media. Even since I stepped down in 1991, the pressure has increased enormously.*

One dimension of it is that the level of fitness required now is awesome. In the 1970s fitness levels in football were stepped up dramatically by Dublin and Kerry, and sooner or later all the other counties and clubs followed suit. When Clare came on the scene in 1995 they raised fitness levels in hurling to a new high. Very quickly other counties and clubs responded in the same way, with heavy training programmes over the winter and so on.

The only sign that all of this may not be necessary was that, when Offaly won the All-Ireland in 1998, apparently they had done little fitness training over the winter. Obviously they trained hard over the summer, but maybe that's a sign that fitness should not be the be-all and end-all. Hopefully they have done the game a service by dispensing the absolute fitness myth. The demands on players now, and on their social lives, are incredible. I can't see how players can get any more fit, and I shudder to think that any more might be asked of them or their trainers.

Quigley saw 1999 as a watershed year in Wexford hurling, 'the swan song for the 1996 team' and time to start building afresh.

I think it's going to be a while before we have a year like 1996 again. To be successful you need to have talent coming through all the time at under-age level, because for every ten that come through as minors only one will make it as a senior. We didn't have that much success at under-age level throughout the '90s, and that's bound to effect us in the short term. I'm not despondent, though, because in 1998 and again in 1999 Wexford did well at Féile, so some of them will start to come through in a few years. The success of 1996 has generated a lot of interest in hurling amongst youngsters and hopefully we should reap the benefit from it, just as Clare have done from their success in 1995.

Whatever about his worries for the Wexford team in the immediate term, Quigley is anxious about the impact of major social changes on the structure of the club.

In rural places especially, I've seen big changes, insofar as the traditional loyalty to the club is weakening. There's a lot more young fellas going to third-level education now, and they are emigrating for the summer and playing hurling in America or somewhere and not in their local club. There's a lot more mobility in the workplace and guys are moving around from place to place, but are generally not willing to travel back to their parish for training every evening, so they are switching to clubs in Dublin or wherever. In the club versus county stakes, the county is winning. Each of these changes on their own are not that significant, but when you add them all together you find they are decimating some of the clubs, especially in the rural areas. I have to say I'm very worried the old-style club may be in danger.

Looking back over his own years on the hurling field, he reckons the greatest character he ever met in the game was Kilkenny's Fan Larkin. 'We had many a tough battle against one another, but he's a great character.'

He selects two other Kilkenny players as his most difficult opponents.

Frank Cummins and Ger Henderson. Frank was Mr Consistency. I'd say the amount of bad games he had in his long career could be counted on one hand. He was not the most skilful player in the world, but he was very strong and competitive and really dictated things from the centre of the field.

The only player I've seen like him in recent years is Clare's Ollie Baker. Although it would be unfair to compare Ollie with Frank, if he keeps going at the same level over a long number of years, I think he could be spoken of in the same breath as Frank.

Asked who he considered to be the greatest hurler never to win an All-Ireland final, Quigley is reluctant to narrow it down to just one.

To come at it from a different angle, I would say that my sympathy is not so much for players who never won an All-Ireland medal, as those who never got the recognition they deserved. I think especially of Paddy Quirke of Carlow. He played with me on the Leinster team but because he was with a weaker county he never got a stage to show off his talents. If he had been with one of the big powers in hurling he would have been a household name.

Kildare's Pat Dunney was another great hurler, if he got the opportunities to really let his talents shine. You need to play at the highest level all the time to develop your talents to the fullest. That's another way players from the weaker counties lose out.

He prefaced his dream team selection by saying that he chose one player although he never saw him playing.

I heard so much about Mick Mackey that he must have been a giant among men. That's why I feel I must select him at centre-forward.

His dream team is:

Noel Skehan (Kilkenny)
Fan Larkin (Kilkenny) Pat Hartigan (Limerick) Eugene Coughlan (Offaly)
Ger Henderson (Kilkenny) Sean Silke (Galway) Iggy Clarke (Galway)
Frank Cummins (Kilkenny) John Connolly (Galway)
Francis Loughnane (Tipperary) Mick Mackey (Limerick) Eddie Keher (Kilkenny)
Kieran Purcell (Kilkenny) Ray Cummins (Cork) Seanie O'Leary (Cork)

THE MIGHTY QUINN

Tipperary came to Croke Park that day armed with a secret weapon in the form of a young full-forward named Billy Quinn. This young hurler's three brilliant goals have really made him the talk of Ireland's hurling circles. His two goals scored in the first half — mark you, he was marked by that prince of hurling full-backs, Diamond Hayden, who was in sparkling form — were masterpieces of anticipation and execution. They made Kilkenny's task in the second half a well-nigh impossible one. His goal after the interval put Kilkenny down for the final count. Undoubtedly this was Billy Quinn's day, and this league final will always be associated with his name.

There is every reason that this young star will go from strength to *strength*. A farmer's son, his daily work on the land takes care of his fitness. A quiet unassuming lad, success has certainly not gone to his head. His only remark after the league final concerned his opponent, Diamond Hayden: 'The cleanest, the most sporting hurler I ever marked.'

The *Sunday Review*'s match report after the National League final in 1954, when raging-hot favourites Kilkenny took on Tipperary and Billy Quinn played the game of his life to assure Tipperary's 3–10 to 1–4 victory on that sultry May day.

A member of the Rahealty club but a native of Rossestown, a couple of miles east of Thurles, Quinn was a prodigious talent as a youngster. He attributes much of his success to his coach at Thurles CBS, a Limerick man, Br Doody. His family background also played its part.

There was a lot of hurling in the family. An uncle of mine, Jack, captained the first Harty Cup winning team.

Quinn played for four years on the Tipperary minors, and has the rare distinction of making his debut in an All-Ireland.

When I was fourteen I was brought on as a sub in the All-Ireland final against Kilkenny in 1950. Tipperary had won all their matches up to then by a cricket score, so I never got a chance to come on and get used to the thing. It was crazy to bring me on for my first match in an All-Ireland final, because I had no idea where I was or what I was doing.

He won his second All-Ireland minor medal in 1953, when he captained the team. One of his team-mates was his brother, Dick. To this day he is a bit blasé about it.

There was no real pressure on me as captain. All I had to do was to call the toss and collect the cup! The only work I had to do was before the All-Ireland final, when our goalie got a panic attack on the way out onto the pitch. The lads called me back and I got him back up against the wall of Hill 16. He was more afraid of me than of the opposition, and he went out and played a blinder.

We were so used to win-ning that I got the cup and threw it somewhere and we went home. There was no cele-bration as such. The big thing was to win the Munster final. There were massive crowds at the Munster finals then. When you came out of the ground your feet would hardly touch the road because there'd be so many people.

The big thrill was to be hanging around with the senior team. The Munster final in Killarney was a classic match, though I'd an awful experience when a Cork man dropped

Niall Quinn (centre) and his father, Billy (left), pose with former top jockey, Tommy Kinane.

*dead beside me with the excitement of the game. The crowd invaded the
pitch a few times and Christy Ring had to escort the referee off the pitch.*

A decade earlier also, such was the intensity of one
Tipperary–Cork match that a man had to be anointed on the
ground. The entire crowd knelt down as a mark of respect.

Within months of captaining Tipperary to the All-Ireland
minor title, Billy was making his senior debut.

*My first senior match was against Laois. It was in the middle of winter
and not a suitable day for hurling. All I remember from the match is
that we got a 21-yard free which was blocked down, but I ran in and
put the sliotar in the net. And the referee disallowed it. To this day I
don't know why. I was disgusted.*

Unfortunately, Billy's inter-county career coincided with a
barren spell in Tipperary's fortunes in the championship.

*We played Cork in 1956 and Seamus Bannon got the best goal I ever
saw, when he ran down the wing and lashed the ball in the net. But
one of our lads threw his hurley twenty yards in celebration, the referee
disallowed the goal, and Cork beat us. It was the greatest injustice I
ever saw in hurling. We got dog's abuse listening in to the All-Ireland
in Thurles that year because everyone was saying, 'Ye should be there if
ye were any good'.*

The year 1956 would be Billy's last in the Tipperary colours. A
taxing job in Boland's Bakery in Dublin, working six days a week
from 7 a.m. to 10 p.m., restricted the commitment he could give to
hurling. He played club hurling for Faughs, but this was not enough
to keep the attention of Tipperary's selectors. Yet, while he played a
few games for Dublin, his commitment to their cause was not total,
and there was always talk of a recall to the Tipp side. This indecision
cost him the opportunity to play in an All-Ireland senior final.

*Dublin had a great team then, with exceptional players like Lar Foley,
Des Foley and Des Ferguson. I thought I was going to go back playing
for Tipperary, but I'm half sorry I didn't pursue the opportunity to
play for Dublin more. They only lost the All-Ireland to Tipperary by a
point in 1961.*

Surprisingly, his star performance in the 1954 league final is not the match that gave him the greatest satisfaction.

I remember playing one league final for Faughs against UCD in O'Toole Park when I was in the late autumn of my career. UCD had a star-studded team and had just won the county final. The match was being played in a gale. Our mentors wanted to play with the wind in the first half but we had a team of 'has-beens' and I thought if they had the wind in the second half they would destroy us.

I was captain and I won the toss and said we'd play against the wind. We got 1–2 in the first half, and they were only 11 or 12 points up at half-time. We brought Jim Prior on for the second half. UCD must have been asking: 'Who are these auld lads?' But the first three balls that went in ended up in the UCD net and we won by eight or nine points.

If I had played with the wind in the first half they would have destroyed us. No match ever gave me more satisfaction. It was better than winning the All-Ireland.

He has no hesitation in naming Christy Ring as the greatest hurler he ever saw. However, he adds a caveat: 'Jimmy Doyle would run him a close second. He could get scores from left or right.'

I think the 1950s were a golden era for hurling, because you had a lot of great teams, like Cork, Tipperary and Wexford. Not only had you great players on all those teams, but go back and you'll find that each of those counties had five or six great players competing for each position.

The best players to actually mark me were John Lyons and Willie John Daly of Cork, Diamond Hayden of Kilkenny, and Billy Rackard and Nick O'Donnell of Wexford.

When I ask him about the game's great characters, he turns straight away to Mick 'Rattler' Byrne.

He was a small man but pound for pound he was the toughest man you'd ever meet. He'd be marking guys from Wexford three or four stone heavier than him, but he'd never be beaten. He was a great corner-back for Tipp, and a wonderful storyteller. He never had much time for all the talk players have today about their injuries, especially about their 'hamstrings'. He always says that the only time in his playing days he heard anybody talking about hamstrings was when they were hanging outside a butcher's shop.

He went to New York with Tommy Doyle, who was making his first flight and was very nervous. Tommy sought comfort from the Rattler who told him, 'Don't be worrying, Tommy. There are two parachutes under the seat. You put one on, jump out, count to ten, press the button, and you jump to safety. What could be simpler?'

'But what happens if the parachute doesn't open?' Tommy asked.

'That's easy,' answered the Rattler. 'You just jump back up and get the spare one.'

Which player has impressed him most since his retirement?

The Tipperary team that came after me were a machine, with players like Babs Keating, Donie Nealon, Jimmy Doyle and so on. Tony Wall was one of the great centre-backs of all time. Tipperary have never really replaced him, and centre-back has always been a problem for us.

Down through the years he has seen major changes in the game. Not all of them have been to his satisfaction.

Hurling has changed a lot. It's become much faster. That time, you'd never lift a ball off the ground unless you were twelve or fifteen yards clear. It was all ground hurling then, but that's died out now.

One thing which pleases him, though, is that the players are much better treated today.

I played once in a championship match against Cork, and after the match I had to go straight home to milk the cows and deliver the milk around town. You were lucky if you got a cup of tea with a slice of lettuce and a tomato. They were so skimpy that you were very lucky to get a new hurley if you broke one.

Although Billy never won a senior county medal in hurling, he won one in football. 'Tipperary football back then was very tough,' he recalls.

At the time you were afraid to be called a coward if you avoided a tackle. So if you were marking a man three or four stone heavier than

you, you ran straight at him rather than around him. I've lost both my
hips since, and I maintain that's how I lost them!

After his performance in the league final in 1954, Billy Quinn
became one of the first recipients of the *Irish Independent*'s
Sportstar of the Week award. In June 1990, his son Niall won the
same honour after scoring the crucial equaliser in the Republic of
Ireland's World Cup clash against Holland, and secured Ireland's
passage into the knock-out phases of the competition. The gloss
was taken off the occasion for the Quinns when a burglar raided
their house as the family went out to celebrate, and stole Niall's
mother's bracelet, which held Billy's two All-Ireland minor
medals.

Billy Quinn is proud of his son's achievement as a soccer player
at club and international level. He recalls that Niall's basic instinct
as a child was to gravitate towards Gaelic games. However, when
he was nine, Niall was sent off in a Gaelic football match and

came home that evening saying, 'I'll never play football again.' The
next approach to him was to play soccer. Who knows what might have
happened if he hadn't been sent off when he was nine?

Like his father before him, Niall Quinn played in an All-Ireland
minor hurling final for Dublin against Galway in 1983. He was
denied a winner's medal, but Billy still muses about the might-
have-beens.

Niall was a lovely hurler because he had a great pair of hands. They
played him out of position in the All-Ireland because they stuck him in
at corner-forward. He had done great damage in the Leinster final
against Wexford, he scored three goals and four points. If they put him
in at centrefield, Galway would've had to put a couple of lads marking
him, and someone else could do the damage. When they brought him out
to midfield, he scored a great point. It was only brought to my attention
a few years ago by a great hero of mine, Jimmy Kennedy, who said it was
one of the best scores ever in Croke Park. The Dublin goalie pucked out
the ball and Niall doubled on it and it went straight over the bar.

Although soccer intervened and claimed Niall's career, his love
of hurling remains unabated.

Niall always has a hurley in his car. He's friendly with hurlers like Nicky English. He paid a small fortune for a hurley signed by Jimmy Barry-Murphy at a charity function, only to discover later that Jimmy hadn't signed it at all! That evening he was trying to get a taxi after the function, but not one would stop for him with the hurley in his hand. Eventually he had to hide it.

Despite his pride at his son's great success in soccer, Billy still feels the game is no match for hurling.

I put my foot in it in 1990 when a journalist came to interview me about Niall after he scored the goal against Holland. When he asked me if I was proud of him, I said without thinking, 'To tell you the truth, I'd rather if he had won a Munster medal!'

His early years might so easily have led that way.

Niall always had a hurley in his hand when he was young. One famous day in Killarney, Babs Keating scored a last-minute goal from a free. That was the day when Donie Nealon came on with a towel and was supposed to have switched the ball, swapping a wet one for a dry one to make it easier for Babs to score. Niall was about five at the time, and he was practising frees in the back garden after the match. My wife, Mary, was doing the ironing, when the window was shattered to smithereens by Niall's sliotar. Mary nearly dropped dead with the shock of the shattering glass. All Niall said afterwards was: 'I was only doing Babs Keating!'

QUIRKE OF FATE

In rural Ireland the GAA is more than a sporting organisation; it is a way of life driven by people rooted in their communities, small parishes with strong personal ties, social traditions and inherited order. Without this understanding, it is not possible to grasp Carlow dual star Paddy Quirke's commitment to Gaelic games. He hurled for the county at senior level from 1974 to 1990, and, disproving former Tipperary great Tony Wall's adage that 'football is a game for those not good enough to play hurling', he played senior football with the county from 1974 to 1987. He played in thirty-one senior county finals, both hurling and football. Yet although he played 106 times for the Carlow hurling team, his immersion in the world of hurling was far from inevitable.

In Dunroe, the townland where I was born, on the outer edges of Bagenals-town, beside Myshall parish, there was no tradition of hurling. My mother was an only child, and my father, a small farmer, never played the game; but I had two aunts who were top-class camogie players.

Tom, Sean, Eamonn and Paddy Quirke.

Camogie was strong there then, so I suppose hurling must have been in my genes. My uncle Packie was a fine athlete as well.

There were seven of us in the family, five boys and two girls. My sisters played camogie with Myshall. We attended a one-teacher primary school in Killoughternane, which was closed in 1966; then we cycled seven miles every day to the De La Salle boys' national school in Bagenalstown. It was Pat Ryan, a Limerick man living in Bagenalstown, who introduced us to the game. My brother, Eamonn, was the first to start playing. We began pucking around at home, first in the farmyard and against the gable end of the house; then we got more organised and erected a goalpost in a field at the back of the house. We were playing with Bagenalstown school team and club then.

At this time Father Phil O'Shea organised a juvenile club in Myshall parish. There was no juvenile club in that area, so the standard was very low, and Father O'Shea got permission from Bord na nÓg to play anyone who had attended Killoughternane school. That included us, so we started to play for Myshall's Naomh Eoin. I can still hear one of Father Phil's chants: 'Keep pulling — it'll have to move.' At this stage, playing under-14, to be beaten by just ten goals was a victory to us.

Our biggest rivals were Michael Davitt's, a parish team from Leighlin, or as we called them, the 'All-Blacks'. We beat them in a minor league final in 1973. It was our first victory and medal. I was marking my best friend and rival, Pat Foley, who was tragically killed in a car accident twenty years ago. We were trailing by a point with a minute to go and it looked like another defeat. I won the ball around midfield and hit a long, high ball into the square. Red Pat Nolan pulled and stuck the ball in the net. That was the start of big things for me.

The upward turn in Naomh Eoin's fortunes continued and they went on to claim four consecutive under-21 championships. However, Quirke was destined for an even bigger stage.

I played my first senior hurling game with Naomh Eoin against Bagenalstown. I was about sixteen at the time and playing in goal. I was terrified! Thankfully I had the three strongest men in Carlow in front of me: Pat Keogh, Brian Fox and Ted Butler. My brother, Eamonn, was midfield that day and marking the legendary Jim English.

In our first senior final in 1973 we were beaten by Ballinkillin. We turned the tide in 1974 by winning the club's first senior hurling title, and we went on to make it three in a row. Naomh Eoin was on the map as a hurling force. I didn't realise at the time what those victories meant to Myshall people. They brought great excitement and life to the village.

I was training Naomh Eoin in 1975 and 1976. In 1975 we were going for the double, but Tinriland beat us in the final. In 1976 we beat Carnew Emmets in the first round of the Leinster Club Championship; St Rynagh's beat us in the second round, 2–16 to 3–9. In 1977 we were beaten at the semi-final stage. That year I was picked on the Leinster Railway Cup team. I was thrilled — I never expected it.

One of Quirke's clubmates was Tom Foley, now famous as the trainer of racehorse Danoli.

Tom Foley played wing-back and centrefield. He was a very good character and a very determined man. Even now, when you meet him, he is much more likely to talk about hurling than horses.

Quirke played for the Leinster football team in both 1979 and 1981, and spent four consecutive years between 1978 and 1981 playing for the Leinster hurling side. Which experience did he enjoy more?

I preferred playing most for the hurlers because I felt more like I was on a par with them than with the footballers. I think I was just one of the lads with them, but it was a bit more difficult with the footballers. In 1979 I played in the Railway Cup final in Thurles against Connacht. I was playing in my favourite position, midfield, along with Ger Henderson. Fan Larkin was the captain. I was marking John Connolly. At that stage I feared no one and I could mix it with the best. I was playing with the best in Leinster — Tony Doran, Frank Cummins, Noel Skehan, Martin Quigley, Pat Carroll, Mark Corrigan, Peadar Carton — and enjoying it.

Hurling was his passport to San Francisco.

I played a few games out there. It was really tough and physical. At one stage I put in my hurley, angled with the bos *to the ground, to block an opponent, and got a severe belt across the face. I was taken off and rushed to hospital. I had no social security cover, but my friends*

decided I would be 'Patrick Foley' — a genuine holder of social security.
The only problem was, when I heard the name Patrick Foley being
called out in the hospital, I forgot that was me and had to be reminded
who I was supposed to be! At that stage I was not in very good shape
and I was expecting some sympathy from the doctor. Instead, all he said
was, 'Were you playing that crazy Irish game?'

His career in Gaelic games had its highs and lows. He
remembers the football county final in 1985, when they drew
against Rathvilly, as 'the biggest disappointment of my career'.

We were a point up and had the game won, but Rathvilly were
awarded a free — when there was no infringement of the rules — on
our fourteen-yard line. Lar Molloy tapped over the free. The ball was
kicked out and the final whistle blew twenty-eight and a half minutes
into the second half. Rathvilly beat us in the replay. I remember saying
to Willie Eustace after that game, 'We are as far away as ever from a
football championship.'

Winning our only football title in 1986, and achieving a rare
double, was a career highlight for me. We were going for the double
again the following year. Éire Óg were the opposition. We were playing
great football half-way through the second half when a bizarre thing
happened. Sean Kelly, the referee, gave Éire Óg a free, and just after he
blew the whistle, I saw an Éire Óg supporter running towards him with
a flagpole in her hand. I tried to bring it to the ref's attention, but he
thought I was complaining about the free, so he ushered me away. The
next second he was floored by a blow from the flagpole.

The game was held up for five minutes while the referee was attended
to, and in the end Naomh Eoin lost by just one point, 2-9 to 2-8.

Rathnure provided the opposition for the second round of the club
championship in '87. We were beaten by one point after being eleven
points up at half-time. I will always remember Eamonn's duel with the
great Martin Quigley that day.

A further highlight of Quirke's career came in 1990, when he
was chosen as a dual All-Star replacement. He marked Eoin Liston
for most of the football game against Kerry, and was stunned when
he was chosen later as man of the match.

As Paddy Quirke takes a nostalgic trip down sport's memory lane, one football game come vividly to mind.

In 1985 we qualified for the National League quarter-final and lost to Armagh in Croke Park, but the game that stands out for me was Carlow playing against Kerry in the Centenary Tournament in 1984. The county grounds were packed. I remember Lar Molloy holding Pat Spillane scoreless, and taking a fine point himself. I was marking Jack O'Shea. We ran them very close, but Mike Sheehy got the vital scores for Kerry in the end.

That Carlow side had lots of potential. Vincent Harvey was training us at the time, and one of his favourite chants was, 'get the ball in around the blue grass area'. Kevin Madden, who is now living in New York, sent me a Christmas card a couple of years ago with a PS: 'Quirke, I'm still looking for the blue grass area.'

How did he assess Kerry, arguably the greatest football team of all time?

Kerry was a team with all the roles. The teams that are most successful are the ones that mould as a team. If a side has one or two great players, you can always blot them out, but you can't blot out six class forwards. You couldn't single out any one player on that Kerry side: they were a team of stars. They weren't just a very skilful side, they always played very intelligently. Mike Sheehy was a player I particularly admired. He was always very cool, never under pressure, and very effective.

Quirke laughs when asked who his most difficult opponent on the football pitch was.

Brian Mullins! He was one tough customer, the sort of fella that you'd rather have playing with you than against you.

He has especially fond words for one of his former clubmates, the late James Doyle, known as 'the Jigger'.

He was a great character. In 1985 we played the Westmeath champions, Brownstown, away in the first round of the Leinster Club Hurling Championship. This was a hard-fought game and a great victory for Naomh Eoin. A few days later, the Jigger was being asked about the pitch, which had been pretty bad to play on. 'Well,' he answered, 'the grass was so long a hare rose at half-time!'

Quirke's dream football team is:

Martin Furlong (Offaly)
Robbie O'Malley (Meath) John O'Keeffe (Kerry) Niall Cahalane (Cork)
Páidí Ó Sé (Kerry) Kevin Moran (Dublin) Martin O'Connell (Meath)
Brian Mullins (Dublin) Jack O'Shea (Kerry)
Matt Connor (Offaly) Larry Tompkins (Cork) Pat Spillane (Kerry)
Colm O'Rourke (Meath) Peter Canavan (Tyrone) Mike Sheehy (Kerry)

He also picked the hurling team he would like to have played on:

Noel Skehan (Kilkenny)
Aidan Fogarty (Offaly) Pat Hartigan (Limerick) John Horgan (Cork)
Mick Jacob (Wexford) Ger Henderson (Kilkenny) Fr Iggy Clarke (Galway)
Frank Cummins (Kilkenny) Paddy Quirke (Carlow)
Johnny Callinan (Clare) Martin Quigley (Wexford) John Fenton (Cork)
Eamonn Cregan (Limerick) Tony Doran (Wexford) Eddie Keher (Kilkenny)

THE MAN FROM CLARE

The Wind is wild to-night, there's battle in the air
The Wind is from the West and it seems to blow from Clare ...
In suntide, moontide, startide, we thirst, we starve for Clare.

Emily Lawless

One of the oddities of the 1984 Team of the Century was that it did not include a single player who had not won a senior All-Ireland medal. But had one been included, the odds are high that it would have been Clare's Jimmy Smyth, who was chosen at top of the right on the centenary team of greatest players never to have won an All-Ireland medal.

Born in Ruan, Co. Clare, on New Year's Day 1931, he first made his mark in St Flannan's College, Ennis, winning three Harty Cups and an equal number of All-Ireland Colleges medals. He played for five years as an inter-county minor, and made his Clare senior debut in a challenge match in Gort at the age of seventeen. His opposite number was the great Josie Gallagher of Galway. 'I learned a few lessons that day,' he says.

For twenty years he was never off the Clare team, and during that period he played for twelve years on the Munster team, winning eight Railway Cup medals. He was also honoured with a coveted Ireland jersey six times.

His home is full of books from the pens of giants of philosophy, from Thomas Aquinas to Bertrand Russell, testimony to the days he spent studying for a philosophy degree at Trinity College. There is little evidence of his glory days as a hurler: it is the achievements of his children which are celebrated in the photographs on the wall.

Which was his greatest game?

It was against Limerick in the first round of the championship in 1953. I scored six goals and four points.

Two years later his biggest disappointment came against the same opposition.

We lost the Munster final to them by 2–16 to 2–6. Not only had we defeated Tipperary and Cork in qualifying, but we also beat Wexford in the Oireachtas final the previous October in front of 30,000 in Croke Park. Losing to Limerick was a massive blow to Clare and took us a long time to recover. If Clare had won in 1955, I believe we would have won several All-Irelands.

Why did Clare have to wait for Ger Loughnane to take over the team to make the breakthrough in 1995?

We had great teams in the forties and all the way up to the eighties, but it was always the same old story: good management and back-up, commitment in training, but no delivery on the big day. Even on the days when we did deliver, as we did, for instance, against Cork in Killarney in 1986, it was the same old story. You could say it was almost a fear of winning, and sheer bad luck.

There were so many great players in Clare who would have won several All-Ireland medals if they were with other counties. Our predicament was that we had good hurling teams which were saddled with the sorrows of past years. Clare's record was poor and we had no tradition of winning. When you have a tradition, it seeps into the bones and the psyche. It breeds confidence, makes a winner out of a loser. A fair team with a good tradition would always be confident of winning against a better Clare side.

In the past, even the language of the supporters carried the wail and woe of what was said and unsaid. I hated the question, 'Will ye win?' People knew the answer to the question when they asked you. What they were saying was: 'We want you to win, we know you can; but you won't.'

We have broken that barrier at last. Winning and losing will never be the same for Clare hurling in the future. It's strange, but I felt more peace than euphoria after we broke through in 1995, because the weight of the losses of previous years had been lifted off our shoulders.

The win brought esteem back to Clare hurling. In hurling circles, a Clare hurler now means something — no question marks. 'We were All-Ireland champions, and we couldn't believe it,' he continues.

We tested the locked gate for eighty years, but the gate stood firm. We tested it again on the eighty-first year and to our amazement the gate opened. It was a fairy wand that wove happiness and contentment over the county and its people, at home and abroad. When Anthony Daly raised the cup, I realised that the win was bigger than one person. It was more than self-fulfilment, more than seeing the net shaking, more than the exuberance of fitness and health. It was on a place far higher than this. It was a totality: the merging of a collective spirit, a unification of minds that included every man, woman and child of a county unit at home and abroad. It brought life into the people and it was good to be alive.

Jimmy Smith kneels beside Christy Ring before the 1955 Railway Cup Final, with the other Colossus of the game, Mick Mackey, on the far right.
Back (L–R): *Phil Purcell, Pat Stakelum, John Doyle, John Lyons, Gerry O'Riordan, Dr Des Dillon, Tony Reddin ('the best goalie of all times'), Jim (Tough) Barry, Mick Mackey.* Front (L–R): *Donal O'Grady, John Hough, Jackie Greene, Willie John Daly, Josie Hartnett, Jimmy Smyth, Christy Ring and Vincent Twomey.*

Jimmy's words are immortalised on stone in an Ennis sculpture dedicated to the hurling heroes of 1995:

Hurling is special
the body and soul of a people
surviving to speak of a past that is noble, distinctive and proud
with a game that is surely unique.

Behind the hurler and philosopher lies a deep commitment to his native county. The GAA symbolises this depth of feeling.

The GAA achieved three very different purposes. It encouraged local patriotism; it inculcated among its members an uncompromising hostility to foreign games; and it revived local and national pride. Its philosophy is that love of country draws its strength and vitality from love of neighbours, fellow-parishioners and fellow countrymen and women; from love of the scenes, traditions, culture and way of life associated with one's home place; and that a club or county provides a sense of importance, belonging and identity, shared goals, pride and purpose. All the texts are equally charged with such values and aspirations.

Jimmy Smyth explored these aspirations in his book on the ballads of Clare.

The ballad makers write about hurling and the ash, the glory of Munster final day as a symbol and inspiration to the Irish nation; about hurling and football and their association with the land, the sea, the plough and the spade; and the atmosphere of All-Ireland day. They write with feeling about the role of the priest, the transience of life, belief in a God and the power of prayer. All these assumptions are woven into a complex web of understanding. They are content in the knowledge that they have great games, great heroes, great people and great places. They tell us who we are, where we come from, and where we stand.

Jimmy himself has penned a ballad on the game he loves so well. The final verse says it all.

Hurling is old, as old as the hills
And tough as the rocks that lie under.
Hard as the metals that smoulder within

A simmer of passion and wonder.
Hurling is part of the soil and the land
A mixture more polished than gold
And comes to the surface expressive and free
As a skill that is daring and bold.

In 1999 he won the prestigious Clare Person of the Year award.
'It was a great honour,' he says.

It never crossed my mind that I would even be considered for such a
prestigious distinction.
I was reminded of a story my uncle used to relate, regarding a
fellow who couldn't get out of bed in the morning. He made a firm
resolution that this would be rectified, and employed the services of a
landlady, who assured him that in the future he would be called at 8
am sharp in the mornings. The 'prime boys', as my uncle called them,
heard of this and blackened his face with shoe polish when he was
asleep. The landlady was true to her word and called him promptly at
eight. He got up immediately, looked at his face in the mirror and said,
'Good God, 'twas the wrong man she called' — and he jumped back
into bed again. The polish was used so liberally the night I got my
award, I didn't recognise myself either!

He himself is liberal in his praise of the greats of Gaelic games,
like Nicky Rackard,

a great character and in my opinion the third best hurler of all time,
behind Christy Ring and Mick Mackey. Although he became addicted
to alcohol, he had the courage to tell the whole country about it, and
tried to get people to stop abusing drink.

There were a lot of great characters in Clare hurling.

Our goalie at home, Christy, had a great puck out, and back then the
sliotar was much heavier than it is today. We grew up in Ruan, which
is about six miles from Ennis and eight miles from Doora, but Doora
might as well have been in South Africa, because it was too long a
distance for us to travel at a time when no one had a car. I asked
Christy once what was the greatest puck-out he had ever struck. 'If I had
the ball they have today,' he answered, 'I'd drive it to fuckin' Doora.'

There was a man in Ruan who was a great admirer of mine. One day I was bearing down on goal in a very tense match, and the harder I ran the more the Ruan crowd was getting excited. They were calling out all kinds of suggestions about what I should do. Then, just as I was trying to gather my concentration, I heard my number one fan roaring out over the din, 'Take no notice of them, Jimmy. Make your own arrangements.'

Jimmy Smyth has no time for dream teams or for men of the match awards. 'Jack Lynch told me once that those sort of awards are a lottery. There were too many great players to pick a dream team. Des Foley, for instance, was a great midfielder because he was never beaten.'

Since his retirement Smyth has seen many changes in the game.

Forward play has deteriorated since my time, but back play has come on a lot. They mark forwards so tightly now you can hardly do anything. I wonder how Ring would cope now? He would still get a lot of scores, but I think he wouldn't have got quite so many.

Ring was like Muhammad Ali. He once said, 'modesty is knowing where you stand'. He always knew. If he thought he had played below his own high standards, he would be the first to say so. He was well aware of his own ability and didn't believe in concealing the fact that he knew it. I remember we were playing in a Railway Cup match once and he said to me, 'When I get the ball you run in for the pass. And remember, I don't miss.'

Ring held Smyth in high regard also. 'He was talking to my mother one day, and when he was leaving he just said, "Your young lad is a great hurler."'

At an early age, Smyth was given a lesson in the value of having a positive attitude.

I was thirteen when I played my first senior game for St Flannan's in the Harty Cup. I was left half-back and marking a guy who had been an inter-provincial player the year before. He had two points scored in the first three or four minutes. Then I saw a black form approaching me — it was Monsignor Dr Maxwell, and he said to me, 'Jimmy, you're beating the Dickens out of him.' He said nothing else. I thought to myself, 'God, I must be really holding him.' And for the rest of the match I never gave him a puck of the ball.'

FAMOUS SEAMUS

Seamus Bonner played his first match for Donegal in a challenge game when he was just eighteen. His first competitive match came in a league fixture against Louth in Drogheda, starting an unbroken record of service with Donegal which ran until 1985. For the first eight years he was a star midfielder, but as he got a bit older he moved closer to the goal, and the latter part of his career was as a full-forward.

The turning point of Bonner's career with Donegal came in 1972:

> *We played Leitrim in the league in Carrick-on-Shannon. I think the score was 4-13 to 1-3 in Leitrim's favour. Brian McEniff was player–manager of Donegal at the time, and he got us into a room in a hotel in Carrick-on-Shannon and said, 'Right, boys. Today was the lowest we could possibly go. The only way we can go is up. The championship is coming up soon: are we going to make an effort for it or are we not?' We made a vow there and then that we would all train hard for the championship, and we did.*
>
> *We beat Down after a replay, and Tyrone in the Ulster final. It was a fairy tale after so bad a start to the year. As it was Donegal's first ever Ulster title, the*

Seamus Bonner in pensive mood.

*whole county went wild. It was like winning the All-Ireland. We had
a great week afterwards, and the celebrations probably affected us in
the All-Ireland semi-final against reigning champions Offaly. We
were playing very well up to half-time, but we gave away a very bad
goal to Kevin Kilmurray. Even though we lost we were probably
happy enough with our performance, because Ulster teams weren't
doing well in Croke Park at the time. I'd say Offaly got a bit of a
shock that day.*

Donegal were brought to earth with a bang the following year
when Tyrone beat them in the first round of the championship.
'Tyrone were a coming team and went on to win the title,' Bonner
recalls, 'and Ulster was always a graveyard for reigning provincial
champions. I played that day, but earlier that morning I had buried
my grandmother, which is not the sort of preparation you should
have for a big match.'

Donegal were back on the glory trail in 1974, with Bonner in
the forefront.

*In the Ulster championship we beat Armagh and then Monaghan in
the semi-final. We beat Down in the Ulster final in a replay. In the
second half we were eight points down with about twenty-two minutes
to go, but we were lucky enough to get two penalties. I took both. There
wasn't much pressure on me for the first one because we were eight
points down, and I thought if I scored it would make the score
respectable, but if I missed we were getting hammered anyway and it
didn't matter much. There was much more pressure on me for the
second one, because we were three points down and it was to tie the
match. My technique was to get it on target and hit it as low and hard
as possible. Thankfully, both penalties went in and we got another goal
in the last few minutes to win by three points.*

By a strange coincidence, Donegal also got two penalties the
next time they won the Ulster final, in 1983.

*We had nine barren years after 1974. Brian McEniff stepped down as
player–manager and there were a lot of changes on the panel and in the
backroom personnel. In 1977 Derry gave us an awful hammering in
the Ulster championship, and a lot of the old team retired. A few of us
kept on going.*

One of the new players that came on the scene in the mid-1970s was Packie Bonner. I played with Packie at midfield against Sligo. He was about seventeen at the time and he had the offer of going to Glasgow Celtic, and I remember him asking me, 'Seamus, what do you think I should do?'

I told him, 'If Celtic offered me a contract, I'd be gone in the morning.' He went and the rest is history. Despite his success with Celtic he stayed close to his GAA roots and trained with us many times in the summer months. He's still a huge fan of the Donegal team.

Donegal qualified for the Ulster final against Monaghan in 1979,

but they beat us well. The match is best remembered for an infamous incident. The referee threw in the ball. I won possession, sent in the ball to the forwards and one of our lads popped it over the bar. The only problem was that the band were still on the far side of the pitch and they were playing the National Anthem! The referee had to re-start the game and our point was disallowed.

Bonner continued to play with the Garda team in Dublin, along with Eugene Sheelin from Louth.

Eugene was very friendly with Louth star Benny Gaughran, who was playing his club football with Civil Service, and he persuaded both of us to join the club. We got to the county final in 1979. Although we lost it, we won the following year.

His home county got a massive boost in 1982 when Donegal won the All-Ireland under-21 title.

We picked up a lot of new players, like Anthony Molloy, Martin McHugh and Joyce McMullan. We had a nice mixture of young blood and experience. To add to the factors in our favour, Brian McEniff was back in charge of the team.

We were fortunate again to get two penalties against Cavan in 1983, when we won the Ulster title again. I scored a goal from the first one, but there were was only a minute to go for the second and we were three points up, so I tapped it over the bar for an insurance point.

Although Bonner won three Ulster championships, Donegal failed each time at the penultimate stage.

It is always disappointing to lose when you are one step away from playing in an All-Ireland. The biggest disappointment was losing to Galway in 1974. We were very unfortunate. Galway raced into the lead but we pulled them back. I was playing good football, but after about twenty-five minutes I had a collision with Gay Mitchell and had to be carried off. I was no sooner in the dressing-room when Brian McEniff came in with a split thumb. I always feel that was the semi-final that got away, because Galway only beat us by a few points, and if it wasn't for those injuries I think we would have won.

In 1972 we hadn't really expected to win. We had achieved our main goal — to win an Ulster title — and I suppose at the back of our minds we had settled for that. 1983 was a big disappointment also because I knew it was probably my swansong at that level, and my chance of playing in All-Ireland final was gone.

I continued for another two years, until Monaghan beat us in the Ulster championship. They were a very strong side then, with some great players, especially Nudie Hughes, who was a class player and very versatile. Few people could win All-Stars as a corner-back and as a corner-forward the way he did. At that stage I was thirty-five, and though my mind was telling me what to do, my body couldn't keep up with it.

In 1989 Brian McEniff took charge of training Donegal once more and invited Bonner to be a selector. Bonner accepted readily, despite the fact that it committed him to extensive travelling from his Dublin base to Donegal. McEniff's Midas touch was quickly in evidence, and the following year Donegal won the Ulster title. What was the secret of McEniff's success, and what was he like as a player?

As a forward he's the sort of guy I would really hate to have marking me. He was very tough and tenacious. He'd be standing on your toes almost and wouldn't give you much time on the ball.

His dedication is total. Although he's got his own business, if he heard a Donegal man was playing football in Cork he'd drop everything and travel down to Cork to see him play. He never missed a single training session in the 1992 campaign and this encouraged the players to do the same. His will power rubbed off on the players. He's got incredible enthusiasm, and that's infectious.

The Bonner-McEniff double act had its finest hour in 1992 championship campaign, though controversy erupted about Padraig Brogan's appearance in the All-Ireland semi-final.

Padraig had made his name with Mayo, but had declared for us a couple of years previously. He played for us, then he switched back to Mayo. When Mayo brought him on against us in the All-Ireland semi-final, it lifted our lads. Although we were playing poorly, when our boys saw him coming on it made them more determined than ever not to lose the game. The sight of Padraig coming on the pitch caused them to up a gear.

In conversation with this writer, Padraig Brogan candidly admitted that his arrival on the pitch was a serious tactical blunder. As for his reason for transferring back to Mayo, all he says is that 'blood is thicker than water'.

Now on their way to Croke Park to meet Dublin, Bonner's inside knowledge of the capital's players proved invaluable. 'Having played club football so long in Dublin, I knew the Dublin players better than McEniff did. One of the highlights of my career had been captaining Civil Service to the Dublin championship in 1980.

Basically I was keen that we would do two things in the All-Ireland. Firstly, that we would keep very tight on Vinnie Murphy. I knew he was their target man, and if we kept him quiet the other Dublin forwards would struggle. It was also vital that we curbed the Dublin half-back line — we didn't want the likes of Keith Barr running at our defence with the ball.

We had been so unimpressive in the All-Ireland semi-final against Mayo that nobody gave us a chance against Dublin. I think that gave the Dublin players a false sense of security. The media really built them up, and I think the Dubs started to believe their own publicity. That's a dangerous game — something similar happened to Kildare in 1998. In contrast, there was no hype about us, because we hadn't done anything to deserve it. None of our fellas were going on radio shows blowing our own trumpet.

Donegal's All-Ireland triumph over red-hot favourites Dublin sparked off unprecedented celebration in Donegal. The victory came with a price tag for Bonner.

The hardest part of my time as a selector came in the run-up to the final. Tommy Ryan had played for us in the All-Ireland semi-final, but we felt that Manus Boyle could do a job for us on the day. He scored nine points in the final, so our judgement was vindicated, but it was incredibly tough to have to tell Tommy that he was going to miss out.

McEniff and Bonner gave leadership from the sideline, but who were the Donegal leaders on the pitch?

We had four of them in 1992: Anthony Molloy, Martin McHugh at centre-forward, Tony Boyle at full-forward and Martin Gavigan at centre-back. Molloy was a superb leader. He could catch a ball in the clouds and that would lift the team. If you could get past Martin Gavigan you were doing well. Tony and Martin could get you a score from nowhere. After his success with Cavan, Martin is seen now in Donegal as the man who can lead the team back to glory. He would be the people's favourite if he wants the pressure of being a county manager again.

After Brian McEniff and his selectors stood down from managing Donegal — 'We had taken the team as far as we could; they needed a fresh approach,' Bonner remarks — he went into club management in Cavan with Bailieboro.

I was there three years and we won a county final and got to the Ulster final, which we lost because of a controversial refereeing decision. We also won the league twice.

Subsequently, he managed the Leitrim team for a year.

For a small county with limited resources, they are the most amazingly dedicated bunch of players you could ever meet. If you said to them to run up a mountain three times, they would do it without saying a word. I couldn't praise them highly enough. They were great men to train. They just hadn't the resources of a strong squad.

He enjoyed the experience of county management, 'but the travel was awesome. You had to be there at training three or four nights a week, and a lot of weekends you were away from home.'

Dublin is home for Bonner, who keeps in close contact with Donegal fans living in the city.

We congregate in the Portobello pub, which is run by Jamsie O'Donnell, Daniel's brother. If you want to know anything about anyone in Donegal, Jamsie's your man. If he doesn't know you, you're in big trouble.

Who was Bonner's most difficult opponent?

Definitely Down's Colm McAlarney. He was always seen as a great footballer and stylist, but what was less appreciated is that he was also a top-class athlete and a very tough guy to mark. When I moved into the forwards, Monaghan's Gerry McCarville was a very tough man to get around. Humphrey Kelleher of Cork was like that as well.

Although he admired Sean O'Neill and Pat Spillane, there was no contest when asked to nominate the best player he ever saw.

Offaly's Matt Connor was the best. He had it all: brilliant from frees and brilliant from play, and he could do it with either foot. I know him well through working in the gardaí together. It was such a shame that his career ended so early.

The greatest player never to win an All-Ireland medal was also the greatest character he ever came across: Frank McGuigan,

one of the most stylish, exciting and best players around during my career. He was without doubt one of the greatest players never to win an All-Ireland medal. He had a mighty stand and catch. He once scored eleven points in an Ulster final, seven with one foot and four with the other.

I was chosen as a replacement All-Star for Jimmy Keaveney in 1975. All I can say about being with Frank McGuigan on the trip was that it was an education. I can't elaborate further, on the grounds that it might incriminate all of us! That All-Star tour was one of the highlights of my career and the trip of a lifetime.

He chuckles at the memory, but over his lengthy career Bonner was involved in some bizarre events.

I was playing against Monaghan one day in a league match in Ballybofey and I was soloing with the ball twenty yards out from the goal with the defence beaten. I had goal on my mind but I had my

mouth open, and a fly flew into my mouth and I swallowed it and
nearly choked. I was clean through and came to a sudden staggering
stop, and with nobody near me I let the ball fall out of my hands. The
Donegal fans didn't know what happened. I'm not sure what they were
thinking, but I'm sure it wasn't complimentary. The moral of the story
is, when you're on a football field you should keep your mouth shut!

Bonner's dream team is:

Martin Furlong (Offaly)
Robbie O'Malley (Meath) Seamus Quinn (Leitrim) Robbie Kelleher (Dublin)
Páidí Ó Sé (Kerry) Glen Ryan (Kildare) Pat O'Neill (Dublin)
Brian Mullins (Dublin) Jack O'Shea (Kerry)
Matt Connor (Offaly) Frank McGuigan (Tyrone) Pat Spillane (Kerry)
Colm O'Rourke (Meath) Sean O'Neill (Down) John Egan (Kerry)

THE PRINCE OF FULL-BACKS

The annals of the GAA hold a special place for the great players whose genius on the field claims permanent space in the memory of all who love the game. Every county has furnished its stars. At the top of the list of Louth immortals is Eddie Boyle, an outstanding full-back for Louth and Leinster. He played for Leinster between 1935 and 1948, winning five Railway Cup medals; he won Louth Senior Football Championship medals with Cooley Kickham's in 1935 and 1939, and a Dublin Senior Football Championship medal with Sean McDermott's in 1947.

In 1932 he made his debut in a Louth jersey with the county minor side. He was a member of the Louth junior team that reached the All-Ireland final in 1934, but after the semi-final he was promoted to the senior team and was, therefore, ineligible for junior grade. However, he was awarded a medal when Louth won the final that year.

Many years after his playing days had ended, he became Louth's first All-Star when he was nominated for the All-Time All-Star award in 1990. Born in picturesque Greenore in the Cooley peninsula, spiritually he has never left his roots. Shaking hands with this big man at his home in Dublin, which is named Greenore, it is impossible to believe he is in his eighty-seventh year.

*Eddie Boyle
contemplates high balls
and epic tussles.*

The archetypal gentle giant, nothing ever phased him on or off the pitch, until the sad death of his wife in 1997. Given his height, strength, fetch, mobility, anticipation, positional sense and his long accurate kick from hand or ground, he was the complete full-back, though as a youngster he scored thirty points at centre-forward. He played full-forward for Louth once, too, in a challenge game against Monaghan.

Working as a driver for Boland's Mills, he rose at 6.30 a.m. six mornings a week to deliver bread to Wicklow. This routine left him little time for training, but he compensated by playing a lot of matches.

> *For many years I played with Sean McDermott's in Dublin, with my Louth colleagues Kevin Beahan and Jimmy Coyle. I played forty-eight Sundays out of the fifty-two. I often played with the club in the morning and lined out with Louth in the evening. We played and beat Dublin in the Leinster final in Navan and that evening I was due to play with 'Sean's' against St Mary's, Saggart, in the Dublin championship. After the Navan match I thought it would have been inadvisable to have a big meal, so I settled for a glass of milk. I felt like 'a million' when I lined out with the club — I remember never having felt in such good fettle for a match.*

The highlight of his inter-county career came in 1943 when he won his first Leinster Senior Football Championship medal. Boyle was the spine of the team, along with Jim Thornton at midfield and the classy Peter Corr in the forwards. In the Leinster semi-final Louth trailed Offaly by four points, but with his bucket-like hands catching virtually everything Offaly could throw at him, Boyle and his fellow backs kept them to a solitary point in the second half, while the Louth forwards notched up 1–7 to win comfortably. In the Leinster final against Laois, Laois only managed two points in the second half, while such was the service to the forwards that the final margin in Louth's favour was fifteen points.

Louth subsequently lost the All-Ireland semi-final to Roscommon, though Boyle had the consolation of keeping the late, great Jack McQuillan scoreless for the sixty minutes. His second Leinster medal came in 1948, the year Cavan thwarted their All-Ireland hopes in the semi-final.

Neither of his Leinster victories ranks as his most memorable match, he says.

I will always remember a National Football League match against Cavan in the Athletic Grounds in Dundalk. The grounds were packed: Cavan were All-Ireland champions and it was their first game after they won the title in New York. Cavan were hot favourites to win, as we were having a bad time, but it was a sizzler of a match and we played some inspired football, and we won by two points. The town was talking about the match for days afterwards.

He commanded great respect among his peers. When he retired his Louth colleagues presented him with a magnificent gold watch inscribed with the words, 'To a great player — from all Louth footballers.'

Louth goalkeeper Sean Thornton once said that when he played with Eddie Boyle he often felt like bringing a chair as he could just sit down on the goal-line. The great Mayo forward, Eamonn Mongey, said of him:

It was immaterial how the ball came to him. High or low, left or right, carried or kicked — Eddie invariably collected it. Sometimes he came bursting through with it, sometimes he came through side-stepping like a bullfighter to avoid the forwards' rushes, but he came away to clear it. And when Eddie Boyle cleared the ball, it stayed cleared for quite a while!

While Eddie Boyle was chosen on the centenary team of players who never won an All-Ireland, his former clubmate at Sean McDermott's, Paddy O'Brien of Meath, was chosen at full-back on the Team of the Century. Asked how he compared with Eddie Boyle, O'Brien said, 'Eddie was undoubtedly the greatest, and you could put me somewhere at the bottom of the league table.'

Eddie Boyle was a good friend of the late Paddy Kennedy of Kerry and he still has a close bond with Peter McDermott of Meath. 'I really liked playing against Meath,' he says. 'There was always great football between us.'

The football was great, and at times also it was very muscular. Eddie remembers a club match on a dark winter's day when the referee did not show up, so one of the few people attending the game was press-ganged into service. He did so on one condition, that he could assemble all the players in the centre of the field and address them before the match. His terms were readily agreed to and the players were duly assembled in the downpour, bemused looks on their faces. The new referee's message was short and simple. He held up his whistle and said, 'Do ye see this yoke, lads? I'm going to blow it now and blow it again at the finish, and whatever happens in between ye can sort out yerselves.'

Boyle never won an All-Ireland medal, but did not allow that disappointment to diminish his enjoyment of the game. He acknowledges,

> *I was always playing to get into an All-Ireland final, and if I had succeeded in getting to it, I would certainly have been playing for a medal. But I always enjoyed the game so much, that was what was important. Yet, while saying that, I don't mean that I wasn't always all out to win.*

He is a strong believer in sportsmanship, and convinced that forwards can be prevented from scoring without infringing any of the rules.

> *At the very longest, it's only a very short period, really, that you'll be playing the game, so it should always be played properly for everyone's enjoyment.*

Who was his most difficult opponent?

> *I always thought that Kerry's Charlie Sullivan, whom I played against mostly in club games, was a very dangerous forward, and Mayo's Paddy Moclair and Gerald Courell, too, was a great attacker, as was Tommy Murphy of Laois.*

The fear of inadvertently leaving out any great player prohibited him from selecting his dream team, though he singles out for special mention Paddy Doherty and Sean O'Neill from Down, and Meath's Paddy O'Brien.

Special plaudits, too, go to Mick O'Connell.

> *I remember seeing him in Croke Park, kicking out of his hands from sixty yards and scoring a point. It was the greatest score I ever saw.*

Maurice Fitzgerald has the skills to remind me of O'Connell sometimes.

And he describes it as 'a football education to see the way that Sean Purcell used every ball to the best advantage.'

He has noticed one major change in football today when it is compared with the football of his era.

I think a lot more teams have a lot more method in their football nowadays. There were games just as good when I was playing, but more use is made of the ball now.

However, he points out that 'You do get matches where it is quite the reverse.'

He is disappointed by some of the razzmatazz which has become attached to the game, like the trend of celebrating goals as extravagantly as soccer-players. For Eddie Boyle, the game was the thing.

I loved being in the action. When the ball was up at the other goal I was longing for it to be at my end, even if it meant danger. There is one thing you need in any position and that's anticipation. My intention was always to close down all traffic to the goal. You cannot afford to allow things to develop in the play, otherwise anything can happen and you are in trouble. I was always blessed with good anticipation, and in playing full-back I was never relaxed. I was always on my toes even when the ball was way up the field.

My biggest asset was my ability to read the game. I never knew how I knew where the ball was going, but I did. I'd be going out to the ball like a bullet. If you waited, the other fella had as good a chance as you of getting it. That's why I never looked for my man at any time, the ball was all I was interested in. When the ball came in, my man was looking for me, but I was already clearing the ball.

THE DAY THE CROSSBAR BROKE

As a boy, Aidan Brady dreamed of playing in an All-Ireland final. Like so many of his generation, he was converted to Gaelic games by the voice of Mícheál O'Hehir, whose commentaries from Croke Park brought the excitement, drama, elation and heartbreak of All-Ireland day into every kitchen in the country. The goalkeeper on the centenary team of greatest players never to win an All-Ireland medal sampled this special atmosphere on only one occasion, when his Roscommon team lost the 1962 All-Ireland to Kerry by 1–6 to 1–12.

The Elphin native first came to prominence with St Jarlath's in Tuam, with whom he won an All-Ireland Colleges' medal. He won four Connacht medals with Roscommon in 1952, 1953, 1961 and 1962. The first of these victories created a sensation when it came at the expense of the great Mayo team led by Sean Flanagan which won All-Irelands in 1950 and '51. Because of a national newspaper strike, many people around the country only heard the result on the Tuesday after the game, and when they did most thought it was a mistake.

Brady also won two Railway Cup medals, but his playing career is probably best remembered for an incident which has become part of GAA folklore. With less than ten minutes to go in the 1962 Connacht final, Roscommon trailed Galway by five points and looked like a beaten side. A Galway forward took a shot and put his team six points up. But as the ball was soaring over the crossbar, Aidan Brady jumped up, hung on the bar, and it broke. There was a lengthy delay while a new crossbar was found, and with the Galway players' rhythm disrupted, Roscommon snatched victory from the jaws of defeat when the game restarted.

One autumn evening shortly before Aidan Brady's death, I asked him what he had intended by swinging from the crossbar.

'There is no proof but that the crossbar breaking was anything other than an accident,' he told me, his eyes bright with mischief.

When I asked him what it was like to play in an All-Ireland final, he gave me an unexpected answer.

For as long as I can remember, I've heard fellas talking about that and trying to describe what it's like. I've read loads of accounts about it. If you really want to know what it's like, the best person to talk to is Jimmy Murray. He's far and away the best I've ever heard on the subject.

Jimmy Murray's pub-cum-grocery in Knockcroghery is one of Roscommon football's spiritual homes, its walls lined with memorabilia from the county's All-Ireland successes in 1943 and

Aidan Brady leads the Roscommon team before the All-Ireland semi-final in 1952, against Meath. He is followed by Frank Kelly, Brendan Lynch, Bill Jackson, Seamus Scanlon, John Joe Nerney, Gerry Scott, J.J. Fallon, Paddy English, Gerry Murray, Bat Lynch, Bill McQuillan, Eamon Donoghue, Gerry O'Malley and Eamon Boland.

1944, including the football from the 1944 final. The football survived a close shave a few years ago, when Jimmy's premises burned down.

The ball was hanging from the ceiling,' he recalls, 'and of course the fire burned the strings. The ball fell down and rolled safely under the counter as it happened, but when the fire-brigade came one of the firemen jumped off and asked me, 'Is the ball safe?' As I was watching my business go up in smoke on that Saturday night, the ball wasn't my main priority! But he came out later with the ball intact. The next day I got calls from all over the place asking if the ball was safe. To be honest, I was bit annoyed at the time that all people seemed to be concerned with was the safety of the ball, and nobody seem to be too bothered about what happened to the shop!

I had always imagined what it would be like to play in Croke Park. You have to be in an All-Ireland final dressing-room to appreciate the tension: you could cut it with a knife. In 1944 Dan O'Rourke, the county chairman, gave his speech. Just as it was my turn to speak, a bicycle boy in a cap came in with a telegram for me. I immediately thought, 'My God, something terrible has happened at home in Knockcroghery.' The address on the telegram was: Captain Murray, Croke Park, Roscommon. Wasn't that a great address to have for a day? It was from my uncle in Belfast and the message was: Roscommon Abú. Win for the West. I jumped up on my seat with the telegram in my hand, and told the lads to go out and win for Roscommon.

You didn't have a kick-around then when you ran onto the pitch, the way you do now; you went directly into the parade. As I walked around I thought of my parents listening to Mícheál O'Hehir on the wireless. Only one or two people had radios in the village, and I heard afterwards that they had to leave the window open at home to cope with the crowds in the yards outside because they couldn't all fit. My mother was the only one not listening! She was upstairs praying for my brother Phelim and me.

It was all the more special because I was captain and I was playing with my brother on the team. I was small but cheeky. Phelim was the athlete. Brotherly love is a great thing, because if anybody started giving me a hard time I would turn around a few minutes later and see Phelim sorting him out!

Aidan Brady's brothers, Tony and Oliver, won minor All-Irelands in 1939 and 1951 respectively.

How big a disappointment was it for Aidan to lose the All-Ireland in 1962?

Of course it was a big comedown. The match itself was forgettable. We were badly hamstrung when Gerry O'Malley had to leave the field through injury. He was the mainstay of our team for so long, at that stage a Roscommon team without Gerry was like Hamlet without the prince.

As a boy, Gerry O'Malley's footballing skills had been honed in a field at home in Brideswell called 'the Grandstand', because it was filled with kids playing football every evening. To this day the field is still known as the Stand. Aidan Brady says,

Gerry was one of the very best players ever to grace Croke Park, and it was tragic that he never won an All-Ireland final. In 1965, though, he finally won an All-Ireland medal when Roscommon won the junior hurling All-Ireland championship. And he was a great servant of his club, St Brigid's. I'd say it was one of the joys of his life when he won a county title with them.

O'Malley's genius on the field has been well documented. What did Aidan Brady think of him as a man?

I think his most attractive quality is his ability to tell stories against himself. Two stand out for me. Gerry was also a wonderful hurler. At one stage he played for Connacht against Munster in a Railway Cup match. At the time, the balance of power in hurling was heavily weighted towards Munster, but Connacht ran them close enough. On the way home he stopped off for a drink with the legendary Galway hurler, Inky Flaherty. Given the interest in hurling in the Banner County, the barman recognised Inky straight away and said, 'Ye did very well.'

'Not too bad,' replied Inky.

'I suppose if it wasn't for O'Malley you would have won,' speculated the barman.

Flaherty answered back, 'Here he is beside me. Ask him yourself.'

Back in 1962, Gerry had to be taken to hospital after the All-Ireland, and he was in a bed beside a man he had never met before. His

*neighbour knew who Gerry was and they got to talking, the way you
do. The next day a fella came in with the newspapers who didn't
recognise Gerry, and his new friend asked him, 'How did the papers
say O'Malley played?'*

*'Brutal,' came the reply — and it certainly left Gerry feeling even
more brutal!*

*When Gerry retired it was a huge blow for Roscommon and I
suppose many of us felt we would never see his like again, but lucky
enough within a couple of years we discovered another great star in
Dermot Earley. The difference between my time and when Dermot
played in his All-Ireland was that Roscommon should have won in
1980. Roscommon really had Kerry on the ropes early on and should
have put them away. They had all that was needed except the self-belief.*

*I believe the 1980 final was lost the previous year. Roscommon
should have beaten Dublin in the semi-final, and though they wouldn't
have beaten Kerry in 1979, the experience would have stood them in
good stead for the following year.*

*I don't really think you can or should compare players from
different eras, and it's not fair to either Gerry or Dermot to compare
one to the other. Both were superb players over a long number of years
and both had tremendous dedication.*

Another Roscommon player of more recent vintage whom
Brady admired was Tony McManus, not just because of his skill
but because of the intelligent way he played the game. Brady recalls
an incident in a county final between McManus's club, Clann na
nGael, and Kilmore. At one point, when a Clann player grabbed
the ball, a Kilmore player called him by his Christian name and
instinctively the Clann player passed the ball to him. Shortly
afterwards the Kilmore man yelled, 'Tony, Tony, pass the ball' as
McManus won possession. Tony swung around and shouted, 'I
wouldn't let you have the ball even if I was playing with you!'

Brady was less than keen on many of the changes in the game,
especially, as he saw it, the cynicism of some modern footballers.
He was also distressed by the effects of the pressure to win games
on young players in sport in general.

Apart from Roscommon players, who was the greatest
exponent of the game Aidan ever saw?

Sean O'Neill was one of the best players I ever came up against. To mark him was nearly impossible because he seldom did the same thing twice. He could feint and dummy with the ball, take a hard shoulder charge, and go on to score a goal or a point. He had no weakness in his game. He had exceptional fielding ability and wonderful control. Off the hands or from frees, he was deadly accurate, and he had two great feet. He was also deceptively strong. It took exceptional concentration and a high level of fitness to stay with him. He was never beaten until the final whistle.

After his football career ended, Brady, who worked in the Botanical Gardens in Glasnevin, went on to become a well-known voice on national radio on Gerry Daly's 'Ask About Gardening.' He died in 1993. I can still feel that heavy cloud of sadness that enveloped me on hearing the news. My abiding memory of him was the answer he made when I asked him how one knew a player had reached greatness.

You know a player is great coming to the end of his career. When he is gone, a great player will never be forgotten. A bad player is one who is not yet gone, but is already forgotten!

THE PLAYER

To the victor the spoils. Fame, if not fortune, is the deserved reward of those who have the good fortune to play for a successful team. However, for great players who line out for the so-called 'weaker counties', celebrity status is much more difficult to achieve. Westmeath's Mick Carley is a case in point.

He first came to prominence in 1955 when he helped St Mary's CBS, Rochfortbridge, win the Leinster Colleges' Senior B Championship. The year after his inter-county debut, he enjoyed the rare distinction of playing with both the minor and senior Westmeath teams on the same day. That came in 1958, in a Leinster championship game against Louth in Páirc Tailteann, Navan.

He offers a nuanced answer when asked about the difficulties of a club player's making the transition to inter-county level.

On the plus side, it was easier to play against county players because it is much faster and there is a lot more skill involved. On the down side, it takes more time to establish comradeship than at club level.

Starting in the full-back position, he quickly established a reputation as a top-class player and was selected on the Leinster Railway Cup team in 1961. At that time, Railway Cup football and hurling were prestigious events, and to be selected was the highest accolade for a player. By now he had blossomed as a centre-fielder, and it was in this position that he reached his heights, when Leinster won the Railway Cup in 1961 and 1962, and reached the final in 1963.

In 1961 also he was selected on the Rest of Ireland team in the annual fixture with the Combined Universities. This remains one of Mick's cherished memories because of the privilege of lining out with and against the cream of footballing talent in the country. In 1966 he was chosen to tour America for the Cardinal Cushing games.

His happiest memory of playing with Westmeath is of beating Dublin in Tullamore in the championship. Which, though, was his best game?

A little old game against Leitrim in Mullingar in the league. I was playing midfield and I 'couldn't put a foot wrong' for the hour.

There were two crushing disappointments in his career.

The first that stands out was not beating Kerry in 1969 in the League final in Croke Park, a game we could have won. The second was the day Laois beat us in the championship in Tullamore. At half-time we were leading by ten points. In the second half they drew level, and then when Noel Delaney scored Laois's second goal, in the dying seconds of the game, I could feel the hair literally standing on my head. I just could not believe it.

Although he never won medals with Westmeath, he feels ample reward for his playing days was the number of people he met.

My favourite character in Gaelic games is Tipperary's John Doyle. We were room-mates in the Cardinal Cushing games in America. In football, the late Big John Timmons of Dublin was a great character, even though he 'did' me out of another Railway Cup medal. Jimmy Keaveney and Meath's Patsy (Red) Collier were great characters, too. I went with Red to the Cushing games. We

Mick Carley brushes his opponent aside.

were walking down a street in Washington one day and we passed
what we thought was just a public house. Red looked in and called us
back. 'Jaysus, come here lads. Ye never saw anything like this.' And
there was a woman up on the bar doing a striptease!

Carley had a nomadic career at club level. He began with
Rochfortbridge-based St Mary's, which was an important focus for
club football in Westmeath. In 1958 he helped them to a county
intermediate championship. He then moved to the Mullingar
Hospital-based club, St Loman's and was the pivotal figure on their
championship winning teams of 1961 and 1963. In 1968 he joined
the Downs Club, then a rising force in senior club football. He
played with them for seven years, during which time they won
five county senior championship titles, with Carley captaining
them to their titles in 1972 and 1974. In 1972 they reached the
Leinster club championship, only to lose to the mighty St
Vincent's of Dublin. In 1975 he moved to his native club,
Tyrellspass, where he ended his playing days. It was there that he
had the most memorable incident of his career.

I was marking Sean Heavin, a man I played with for Westmeath, in a
club match. I was playing centre-forward. I was at the end of my
career, and my legs were going. At one stage the ball came in, about
ten foot in the air. Sean was younger and much quicker than me so
there was no way I was going to beat him. Just as he was about to jump
and claim the ball I let a roar, 'Let it go, Sean!' He stopped and let
down his hands and the ball fell into my arms. The whole field opened
up for me and I just ran through and tapped it over the bar.

When his playing days drew to a close, he put his experience
and guile into managing and coaching Tyrellspass. This exercise
has given him very definite views about what must be done for the
game in the new millennium.

I would like to see a greater input from Croke Park to the schools of
Ireland, in that a system would be implemented to teach young boys in
both hurling and football and to assist clubs in that respect. I don't
think the powers-that-be realise the amount of hard work and sacrifice
that club members perform every week to see that the game is
propagated and looked after.

Who was his most difficult opponent?

I had many of them, the most notorious being Mick O'Connell in 1969. I also had problems with Kerry's Seamus Murphy; that 'big bag of bones' from County Meath, Peter Moore; the late John Morley of Mayo, and others too numerous to mention.

Given his legendary status in Westmeath football, it is surprising to hear that football is not in fact his favourite game.

If I was given a choice between getting tickets for an All-Ireland final in football or hurling, I would definitely choose the hurling final. Hurling is such an unbelievably skilful game, and it's a real man's game. I don't like the way footballers today go down with small injuries, or all the emphasis on psychology in preparing for matches. There's too much nonsense. Footballers have gone softer since my time.

He laughs remembering some of Gaelic games' stranger moments.

A lot of strange things happen in club games, but I think the strangest story I have heard was about a ladies' camogie club match about twenty-five years ago, when Cullion played a man on their team. What was stranger still was that nobody noticed the difference until after the match.

I once played a club match in Offaly against Walsh Island, a club most people will know about because of Matt Connor. After the game was over, I was about to go home when a fella called me over and told me I should stay for a junior match between Clonbullogue and Bracknagh. I didn't really want to but he was adamant that I should stay, so I agreed to stay for five minutes. There was nothing special for the first couple of minutes until suddenly a fracas developed, and then all hell broke loose. Every one was swinging and punching. I found out later that there was a lot of history there.

It took about five minutes for the referee to sort things out and get order back. Another mêlée broke out and then another. I swear that there was no more than five minutes' football in the first half. In fact things were so bad that at half-time the priests from the two parishes went in to try and calm things down.

Things went fine for the first twenty minutes of the second half, and then another scrap broke out and the match had to be abandoned.

Obviously, the man who told me to stay knew what to expect. My only regret is that nobody made a video of the game — it would have made a great comedy.

Asked about the greatest players he ever saw, he chants a litany:

Most of the Down team of 1960 and 1961, Galway's Martin Newell, Offaly's Tony McTague, Dublin's Paddy Holden, both Johnny Egans (Offaly and Kerry), Pat Spillane, Offaly's Sean Foran, Leitrim's Packy McGarty, Sean Purcell, Mayo's Willie Casey, Kevin Heffernan, Armagh's Jimmy Whan and Dublin's Cathal O'Leary.

He prefaces his dream team selection with some qualifying remarks.

I've seen so many great players over the years, I feel guilty leaving them out. It's very hard to leave out the great Gerry O'Malley for the number six spot. We used to play Roscommon every year around Easter for the Railway Men's Cup, and it would take half our team to mark him. He could solo from one end of the field to the other, and nobody might get a hand to him because he was able to dummy and feint so well. He was a big man and he could score a point from fifty or sixty yards.

I have a total respect for every player I met over the years. If they hit me hard and played the game as was, fair and square, you gave as good as you got and we all went to work the next day, lamenting or revelling as was fitting.

His dream team is:

Andy Phillips (Wicklow)
John Bosco McDermott (Galway) Paddy O'Brien (Meath) Johnny Egan (Offaly)
Mick O'Dwyer (Kerry) Paddy Holden (Dublin) Martin Newell (Galway)
Seanie Walsh (Kerry) Mick O'Connell (Kerry)
Tony McTague (Offaly) Paddy Doherty (Down) Pat Spillane (Kerry)
Sean O'Neill (Down) Sean Purcell (Galway) Kevin Heffernan (Dublin)

Subs:
John Egan (Kerry), Sean Foran (Offaly), Pat Mangan (Kildare),
Pat Dunney (Kildare), Charlie Gallagher (Cavan), Martin Furlong (Offaly),
Gerry O'Malley (Roscommon), Packy McGarty (Leitrim),
Willie Casey (Mayo), Jim McCartan (Down), Jackie Whan (Armagh),
Niall Buckley (Kildare) and Michael Donnellan (Galway)

MIDFIELD MAESTRO

Jimmy Flynn was at the centre of the most successful period of Longford's football history. His towering performance at midfield helped the county beat the mighty Galway in the National League final in 1966, and two years later he was outstanding as Longford took its first Leinster senior title. Longford's only previous successes at national level had been in the All-Ireland junior championship of 1937.

A creamy haze wraps itself around the peaks of the Dublin mountains as Flynn recalls his early days. He first made his mark with his native Clonguish, where a formative influence on his style was one of the most famous characters of Longford football, Bertie Allen.

Jimmy Flynn looks the archetypal lean, mean fighting machine.

He was the greatest character I ever came across in football. I remember playing a nine-a-side juvenile match in Longford. Eamon Barden and I were in the half-back line and we were pretty strong, so we were winning a lot of ball and sending it in to the forwards, but they couldn't score. At half-time Bertie said that the four forwards were like Khrushchev, Eisenhower, Macmillan and De Gaulle they were so far apart.

He had a great turn of phrase. All kinds of comments were attributed to him, though I'm not sure if all of them were true!

Success quickly came at schoolboy, juvenile and minor level with his club, a trend which accelerated when he went to the famous footballing nursery, St Mel's College. In 1961 he helped the school reach the All-Ireland Colleges final.

I was playing at midfield, marking John Morley. We lost by a point in front of 15,000 people in Athlone. Apart from having the best from Longford, we had up-and-coming talent from other counties, like Mick Ryan from Offaly and Dermot Gannon, who went on to play for Leitrim and Connacht. His father had been the last man to captain Leitrim to win a Connacht final, back in 1927.

Flynn made his senior debut for Offaly as a nineteen-year-old in 1963, marking Larry Coughlan. That year he won a Dublin championship medal with University College Dublin in a side made up almost entirely of inter-county players, such as Westmeath's Georgie Kane ('a lovely footballer'), Kerry's Paudie O'Donoghue, Longford's Bobby Burns and Sean Murray, who doubled up as team manager. To complete a memorable year, he also won a Longford championship medal with Clonguish. It was one of eight county titles with his native club.

A turning point in Longford's fortunes came when three times All-Ireland winner Mick Higgins of Cavan agreed to become county trainer in 1965. Longford had reached their first Leinster final earlier that year, and though they lost to Dublin by 3-6 to 0-9 after missing a penalty at a crucial stage in the game, that September they won their first senior tournament of note when they defeated Kildare to take the O'Byrne Cup.

The New York-born Higgins found that management was a more frustrating experience than playing. He often told the story of taking charge of Cavan for a championship match against Armagh. As the match reached its climax, Armagh took control over midfield, and Higgins decided to send on a sub, big Jim O'Donnell, whose high fielding was just what Cavan needed. O'Donnell didn't seem to realise the urgency of the situation, though, and after going on to the pitch he strolled back to the sideline in search of the slip of paper bearing his name for the referee. Moments later O'Donnell was back again seeking a pair of gloves. Higgins roared at him to get back to his position immediately and not to mind about the gloves. He ran off, but returned a minute or two later to ask Mick, 'Would you ever mind my false teeth?'

Higgins also managed Cavan at one point during his time with Longford, and a conflict arose when both counties qualified to meet each other in the League semi-final to be played at Carrick-on-Shannon. Mick's first loyalty was to Cavan, so Sean Murray and Brendan Barden took temporary charge of Longford for the semi-final.

Jimmy Flynn has his views:

To win the league was a great achievement for a small county like Longford, and although there was a lot of dedication on the part of the players, I think Mick Higgins has to take a lot of the credit for it. He was never a hard taskmaster in training, but he grew into the job with us. There was always great local rivalry between ourselves and Cavan, but Longford people up to then had never much to shout about in comparison with our northern neighbours. We changed that. He gave us the confidence to do it.

We should have won the Leinster final in 1965. We were a far better team than Dublin on the day, but we had neither the experience nor the confidence and didn't drive home our advantage. I was marking Des Foley, and I remember him telling me later that Dublin had got two very soft goals from speculative balls that went into the square.

Higgins was not the only one responsible for the upturn in Longford's fortunes.

We had a great county chairman. He had a very cool head and was a very astute man. Another key figure was our manager, Fr Phil McGee (brother of Eugene). He had a great love for the game. It was a passion with him, and you need people like that behind you. In 1966, when we were invited to go to America, I remember Fr Phil making a statement which I think he regretted afterwards. 'We'll go to America when we're All-Ireland champions,' he said. We never got there!

Flynn recalls:

There was no such thing as foreign holidays then. You were lucky if you got to stay in a good hotel before a big match. Mick Higgins told us a story from his days with Cavan, when he captained them to an All-Ireland final victory in 1952. The first match ended in a draw, and for the first time the GAA brought the two teams together for a meal after the game. When Mick and some of the Cavan boys got to the hotel they ordered drinks, just bottles of ale and a mineral, and when Mick went to pay for it the barman said it was on the GAA. Mick double-checked to see if he had heard correctly, and when he found that he had, the order was changed to brandies. Well, there was no free drink for the replay!

Flynn does not see Longford's victory over Galway as the defining moment in the county's changing fortunes.

One of the great memories I have of that league campaign was of playing Sligo, who had a very strong team that year. They were a bit like ourselves in that they could have made the breakthrough, especially as they had Mickey Kearins, a fantastic footballer. When Sligo wanted to beat you they dragged you into Ballymote, which was a fairly remote part of the country. For the match, our sub goalie, the late Michael 'Smiler' Fay, was given the job of doing the sideline. Towards the end of the game John Donlon ballooned the ball over the line, and it was as clear as the nose on your face that it was a line ball to Sligo, but Smiler gave it to us. We got a point and stole the match. The Sligo crowd were incensed by that, and rightly so, and when the game was over they were baying for Smiler's blood. Smiler saved a fair few goals for Longford in his playing career, but he saved that match for us. I believe that was the day we won the league.

Galway looked invincible in the build-up to the league final, though they clearly did not regard Longford as pushovers and flew their outstanding half-back, Martin Newell, back from Frankfurt for the game. In the event, Longford won by 0–9 to 0–8. Eight of Longford's points came from Bobby Burns, while Sean Murray got the remaining score. Jimmy Flynn's high fielding and work-rate earned him the man-of-the-match accolade.

He recalls:

There were hardly 5,000 people left in the county the day of the final. When we got home on the Monday evening we were paraded round on a truck. I'll always remember Larry Cunningham, who was at the height of his fame, got up with us and sang a song. Because it was the first time we won a national title, there were ecstatic celebrations in the county. We didn't become Longford's answer to the Beatles, but at least when any of us went to a dance in Rooskey after that we were recognised!

The final was one of those days when you are up for it, and the game went well for me. The one incident I remember most from the game was Martin Newell coming up the field with the ball and hitting a diagonal pass to Cyril Dunne. I intercepted it, with nobody between me and the goal, which was about seventy yards away. There was about ten minutes to go and I was very tired. I soloed through and, with nobody to beat but the goalie, I shaved the post and put it wide. I fell on the ground with exhaustion and I can still hear Jackie Devine saying to me, 'Why didn't you pass the ball to me?' It made for an agonising finish because Galway were throwing everything at us, but our backs held out well.

The joy on the faces of the Longford crowd stays with me. We had a hell of a night in Power's Hotel afterwards and a hell of a day the following day. The party finished on Tuesday — but I'm not saying which Tuesday! We came down to earth with a bang, though, when we lost in the first round of the Leinster championship against Louth. I thought it was unfair to us to have to play a championship match just two weeks after winning the league final.

Having reached the dizzy heights of success, Longford football now found itself shrouded in controversy.

After we won the league we had to play a two-header with New York: one game in Croke Park and the second a week later in Longford. The Croke Park match was a fiasco and ended in an absolute shambles. The Longford fans were livid with the referee because they felt he let the New York lads away with murder. They were very, very physical — journalists told me we should refuse to play them in the second game. A lot of the Longford crowd went onto the pitch to try and get at the

New York fellas after the Croke Park match, and when we played
them in Longford it was the first time they had to put barbed wire
around the pitch.

Happy days returned to Longford in 1968 after they beat
reigning All-Ireland champions Laois in the Leinster semi-final in
Mullingar. Flynn, unfortunately, picked up a knee injury and
missed out on the All-Ireland semi-final against Kerry. 'What really
killed me was losing out on the opportunity to mark Mick
O'Connell.' Longford lost the game by two points.

One of the problems of Longford, and weaker counties generally, is
that we didn't have strength in depth and that told against us in the
Kerry game. We had good players when we were all free from injury,
but couldn't afford to be short of anyone.

We won the Grounds tournament later that year. After that the
team began to break up. Fellas like Bobby Burns, Sean Murray,
Brendan Barden and Sean Donnelly were stepping down.

Flynn retired from inter-county football in 1972.

I was only twenty-eight, but at that stage you were becoming a veteran
when you reached that age. It's hard to motivate yourself when you
know your team is on the way down.

Although his successful property business keeps him in Dublin,
Flynn keeps a close eye on the fortunes of Longford football. He
is a big fan of Dessie Barry, whom he describes as 'a lovely
footballer'.

He was as good a scorer as anyone in the country in recent years. He's
one of those guys that if he was with a stronger county would have a
huge profile.

'Weak counties like us got very little coverage in my day,' Flynn
points out.

I never saw myself on television. At least now Longford have some
promising young players like Paul Barden, who is the best young player
I've seen in many years. He's going to be a big name on the national
stage.

Flynn feels that Gaelic football is in a healthy state, though he believes it could benefit from minor surgery. 'I think the only thing the GAA has to work on is to have the rules applied consistently. The other thing I would like to see is to allow players to pick the ball off the ground. This is where injuries happen, and from a refereeing point of view it would help. I can't see what the current rule adds to the game as a spectacle.

The fitness levels are fantastic now and the dedication is incredible. I don't think training was anything like as intensive then as it is now. Maybe we did a bit more ball play, though, which produced a different type of team.

The best team I saw in terms of excitement was the Down team of the early 1960s. My father worshipped the ground Sean Purcell walked on. When I was young, my father often brought me to see him play, and he was a Colossus. His Galway team of the 1950s were a great team. I'd be doing Longford a disservice if I didn't say the Galway three-in-a-row side weren't a great team also! The great thing about all Galway teams was that they were always very clean and fair. Mind you, they had a couple of hard men, but I'm not going to mention any names! After I retired, the great Kerry team were of course something special.

There is no equivocation when he is asked to name the best player he ever saw. 'Definitely Sean Purcell was the best natural footballer I ever watched playing the game.'

He offers a more qualified assessment of Mick O'Connell.

I played on Mick O'Connell twice. I especially recall a match down in Killarney when we both caught the ball together, and whatever way it happened, I kind of dragged him down and landed on his backside. The next time we clashed I was picking the ball up off the ground and he came in and pulled on me. I said, 'Now listen, Mick, that's not the way the game is played.' But because of the previous incident he said, 'Well, it's better than pulling and hauling.' I remember that remark well, and I kind of laughed.

He took football very serious. I thought he was a purist. He was a complete footballer in that he had all the skills: he could strike the ball off the ground, had a great catch, was a great athlete and could kick with both feet. I don't regard him as a match winner in the same way as I would have seen Jack O'Shea or Eoin Liston — I had great time for 'the Bomber'. I would have a question mark about O'Connell's temperament. It wasn't as strong as other parts of his game. It was possible to psych him out of a match, and the Offaly boys were pretty adept at that.

If you're talking about great footballers, one of the lads I would have to mention is Willie Bryan. We had some great tussles. I met him a few years after we retired and he said, 'I've a great photograph of you and me up in the air catching the ball. We both have of our hands around the ball, but I have mine on the inside!' I thought it was a great remark. He had a great sense of humour and was a lovely footballer.

Who was his most difficult opponent?

Andy Merrigan from Wicklow. He was very strong and a real slogger. Clashing with him was like hitting a brick wall. They talk about Paddy McCormack, who was very tough all right, but not in comparison with Andy Merrigan: he was an iron man.

Football at the time was very tough. When you played teams like Laois and Offaly you always knew it was going to be a physical battle. There was no quarter given. There was quite a lot of tough stuff and quite a bit off the ball. You had to protect yourself.

Apart from his career with Longford, Jimmy Flynn can also look back on a representative appearance with Ireland.

I played for Ireland against Australia in Croke Park, the first time Ireland played Australia. I was marking a famous Australian player called Ron Barrazzi. We put together a team with the likes of Jimmy Keaveney, Tony Hanahoe and Paddy Cullen. We were a motley crew, though in fairness I think it was more a question of who was available than who was the best. My only specific memory of the game was Jim Eivers getting the oval ball and trying to solo it at one stage.

The Australians wore sleeveless black singlets and all of them were bronzed. We were wearing white vests and were all as white as sheets. I reckon there was about seven or eight thousand in the crowd that day, and when we trotted out they started laughing at us because we looked so anaemic in comparison with the Aussies!

Jimmy Flynn's dream team is:

Paddy Cullen (Dublin)
John Egan (Offaly) John O'Keeffe (Kerry) Tom O'Hare (Down)
Páidí Ó Sé (Kerry) Kevin Moran (Dublin) Sean Murphy (Kerry)
Jack O'Shea (Kerry) Brian Mullins (Dublin)
Jimmy Keaveney (Dublin) Sean Purcell (Galway) Sean O'Neill (Down)
Mikey Sheehy (Kerry) Eoin Liston (Kerry) Colm O'Rourke (Meath)

THY KINGDOM COME

The GAA field has been greatly strengthened by Irish rugby. Rugby international Ciaran Fitzgerald played for Galway minors in the All-Ireland hurling final. Dick Spring, whose father, Dan, captained Kerry to All-Ireland football victory in 1940, played both hurling and football for Kerry and might well have gone on to emulate his father's achievement had not rugby beckoned. Kerry's 1981 All-Ireland winning captain, Jimmy Deenihan, also played rugby for Tralee. In a county where football and rugby regularly intertwine, Mick Galwey could have been one of the Kerry greats. Instead he chose 'the road less travelled' and opted for rugby as his main game.

As a boy, his hero was Mick O'Connell.

I came from a football area, Currow, near Castleisland — the same area as Moss Keane came from. I played for them every year from when I was nine until I was thirty-two, when contractual obligations prohibited me. Football was my first love, and after school my interest increased when I started working as a baker with Charlie Nelligan, who was a star with the great Kerry team. I got minor trials with Kerry and played at midfield for them in the Munster minor final in centenary year, when we lost to Tipperary. Three years later we beat them at under-21 level, only to lose the All-Ireland final to a very strong Donegal side.

Galwey reaped the benefit of the internal discord that prevailed in Kerry in the mid-1980s as a result of the team being used for advertising. On the morning of the All-Ireland final in 1985,

Sunday newspapers carried full-page ads showing several Kerry players posing around a washing machine, and the slogan: 'Only Bendix Could Whitewash This Lot'. The controversy blew up again the following spring, when the Kerry players were to be compensated for their modelling venture with a team holiday.

The Kerry team were on strike and they were looking for fifteen lads to go to Tourmakeady in Mayo, so I was brought in because I had played under-21 the previous year. It was a weekend away, and I'll never forget it especially because we all got Aran jumpers after the match, which was great. Then I was called into the Kerry panel for training.

I was nineteen at the time and it was a great experience for me to be rubbing shoulders with Mick O'Dwyer and all these great players, who were not just very talented, but totally committed. I was very impressed by their professional approach and what I learned from them probably stood to me in my rugby career. Every game with them was very competitive, which is not a bad thing.

It was very intimidating going in to train with such great players. The training back then was like the way we train in rugby now: short and sharp. Sometimes lads would get sick in training, but O'Dwyer never managed to make me sick! Afterwards it was a case of us going down to the Imperial Hotel in Tralee, where we used have steaks and chips and onions and a pint of milk. Now it's different and you're not advised to eat like that, but it didn't do that Kerry team any harm.

Mick O'Dwyer had a great way of making things competitive and of getting the very best out of his players. He would get old lads sprinting against young lads on a one-to-one basis: 'wire to wire' it was called. Then it was backs against forwards, which was awesome. Some of the tackling was ferocious; you'd never see anything like it in a proper match, but it really prepared fellas for championship football.

In fairness to O'Dwyer, he really knew when to push and when to rest players. I remember that in 1986 he hadn't really pushed the players too hard up to the Munster final.

Mick Galwey,
football and rugby
star.

After that match he announced that the team were to have a few days off, but that six people would have to return early for extra training. Everyone's ears cocked straight away. Páidí Ó Sé, the Bomber and Seanie Walsh were three of the names. They were all exceptional players but for different reasons probably needed some extra training. I'm at the stage now that they were at then, where you have to train twice as hard just to keep up with the young fellas. I was brought in with them because I wasn't sharp enough just then, and the six of us were given extra laps and push-ups and sit-ups. It was hard work, but it had to be done.

O'Dwyer would pull you aside from time to time and say you were going well or whatever. At the time Jack O'Shea and Ambrose O'Donovan held the midfield places and Dermot Hannafin and I were challenging for them. We were never going to get ahead of them, but we kept them honest. I remember Seanie Walsh saying one time that the contests between the four of us in the midfield were very good.

Galwey could hardly have chosen a more auspicious occasion for his championship debut.

That summer I came on as a sub for the Bomber in the final ten minutes of the All-Ireland semi-final against Meath. It was very thrilling to come on in Croke Park against Meath, who were a 'coming' side, while Kerry were on the way down. It was a baptism of fire, because I went in on Mick Lyons. Mick was a great footballer, of course, but I wasn't two minutes on the pitch when he gave me a dig in the ribs. I was still very nervous, so I swung back at him, but I didn't connect. I have to tell you, he didn't waste time letting me know he was still the main man! Some young fella wasn't going to steal his glory. I played a few times on him after that and he turned out to be a grand fella, but my first introduction to Mick Lyons wasn't the nicest!

I touched the ball once. I caught it and I'll always remember passing it on to Ger Power, who in turn gave it on to Mike Sheehy, but the goalie made one of the saves of the year. I really felt that I was part of the set-up because I had actually played a game.

I injured my ankle coming up to the All-Ireland against Tyrone, and in fairness to Mick O'Dwyer he kept it quiet and carried me along for the final. Having got the taste of Croke Park in the semi-final, it was a step up again to be there for the final. It looked bad for us when

Kevin McCabe stepped up to take the penalty, but after he drove the ball over the bar we got into our flow. I remember Timmy O'Dowd coming on as a sub and playing a stormer, as did Pat Spillane. That was the great thing about that Kerry team — there was always someone who could turn the game for you.

Earlier that year I won a Munster Senior Cup medal with Shannon. Shortly afterwards, Kerry played the league champions, Laois, in a GOAL challenge, and after the match we were going into O'Donoghue's pub when Ogie Moran turned around to me and said, 'Jesus, Mick, you could be the only man to win a Senior Cup medal in rugby and an All-Ireland medal in the one year.' I remember thinking that would be a wonderful achievement if it came to pass.

The following year Larry Tompkins and Shay Fahy put an end to our dreams. A lot of players retired after that, so it was the end of an era. I played for Kerry for a few years after that, mostly as a sub. My main commitment was to rugby, which probably didn't go down too well in Kerry at the time. I do regret not being able to play more for Kerry, but overall I have no regrets about my career.

As acknowledged in the introduction, strictly speaking Galwey's inclusion is outside the book's parameters, but he never got to play in an All-Ireland final.

Galwey has warm memories of the great footballers he played with on that magnificent Kerry team.

They were all great characters. Páidí Ó Sé stood out because he was so committed and enthusiastic. Football was his life. Even back then you knew he'd be the one to keep going and make his mark in management. Tommy Doyle was very funny. Publicly he kept to himself, but with the lads he was great fun. Charlie Nelligan was also a great character.

The young fellas had to show a bit of respect, but there was great craic in the squad too. Dermot Hannafin was a good mimic and great at taking off O'Dwyer. Micko would sometimes be left wondering why the lads were collapsing with laughter, not realising he was being 'done'. The best fun came after training as soon as O'Dwyer left the dressing-room. If somebody got a bit of a bollicking from O'Dwyer, the whole squad would take the mickey out of him.

Galwey missed out on the rebuilding programme after O'Dwyer's departure, because he had opted to devote his energy to rugby. The roots of his interest in the oval ball came from another noted Gaelic player.

> *As Moss Keane was from Currow, he was my hero. There was massive interest in the area when he started to play for Ireland. His first international was a very robust game, and the story goes that Moss's mother was getting very agitated watching the match on television, and she said: 'Poor Moss will break a leg.' His father replied, 'He might, but it won't be his own!'*
>
> *The first time I saw him play, though, was in a Gaelic match in Currow. He was their full-forward and target man and he did the job well, though I think rugby robbed him of his athleticism. Then there was the whole Moss legend, which added to the glamour of rugby.*

According to folklore, after a less than resoundingly successful career as a Gaelic footballer with University College Cork, Moss's conversion to rugby came when he overheard the current GAA press officer, Danny Lynch, remark: 'A farmer could make a tidy living on the space of ground it takes Moss to turn.'

There were other formative influences on the young Galwey.

> *Castleisland had a great tradition of rugby, too, and John Browne there also had a huge influence on my development as a rugby player. It makes me think back to playing for Ireland against Western Australia in Perth in 1994, when I found I was in front of the Prendiville stand, which was called after a fella from Castleisland.*

Notwithstanding his commitment to rugby, Galwey retains a keen interest in the fortunes of his native county. Which of the great Kerry team did he admire most?

> *They all impressed me. The Bomber stood out. He was exceptional, but probably the player that had to work hardest on his game — a bit like myself, if he didn't stay away from the table he put on the pounds. He was one of the players that could turn a game from you. The likes of Pat Spillane, Mike Sheehy and Jack O'Shea probably got more of the limelight, but to me the Bomber was the key to Kerry's success.*

I remember playing an under-14 club match once and the opposition had this eleven-year-old at corner-forward who could do things with the ball that nobody else could. It was Maurice Fitzgerald, and you just knew he was going to be a real star. I was very young then and not a great judge of a player, but I remember saying, 'Jaysus, that guy's amazing.'

The Dubs had a lot of great players at the time, even though we never liked them! Kevin Moran was the one who caught the eye, especially because he made it in both codes. Roscommon gave Kerry some of their toughest matches and you'd have to mention Dermot Earley, who was an exceptional player, maybe the best in my time not to have won an All-Ireland medal. Offaly's Matt Connor was a class act and scored freely against a great Kerry back line, which said a lot about his talent. When Kerry were beating Cork every year in the Munster final the Leesiders had some great players, like Dinny Allen. Kevin Kehilly was probably the only player who could ever have held the Bomber.

In Kerry you are considered to have an inferiority complex if you only consider yourself as good as anybody else, so it comes as little surprise to discover that Galwey's dream team is the Kerry team of the 1970s and '80s. And he feels that most of that team could also have been great rugby players.

You could slot all the great Kerry players into positions on the rugby pitch. Jack O'Shea was a natural athlete and a powerful player, who would have made a great number eight or flank-forward. The Bomber would have been a good second row. Mike Sheehy would have been a natural out-half. Páidí Ó Sé would have been the perfect prop-forward, in the Peter Clohessy mould!

Galwey feels that his training as a Gaelic footballer was a big help to his rugby career, primarily in terms of having an eye for the ball. But he says, tongue in cheek, that the real benefit of his Kerry associations did not come on the playing field. The best thing of all is that Galwey has never incurred Mick Doyle's wrath.

In his weekly column in the *Sunday Independent* former Irish rugby coach Mick Doyle airs his views on the state of Irish rugby, often in such trenchant terms that Moss Keane once said to him:

'Thanks be to Jaysus I don't play any more. Otherwise I'd be afraid to open the paper on Sunday!'

The best help my Kerry roots has been to my rugby reputation is that Mick Doyle has never written anything critical about me, unlike other second-row forwards that people could think of! In Kerry, it's a bit like the Mafia. Come hell or high water, we always stick together.

ON A WING AND A PLAYER

To a generation of Roscommon fans like me, Johnny Hughes was a real pain in the butt. As the linchpin of the Galway defence throughout the 1970s and early 1980s, he was the rock on which wave after wave of Roscommon attacks perished.

Born into a family of fourteen in Mountbellew, the great wing-back surprisingly never played for the Galway minors. He did, however, play at under-21 level for three years, and in 1969 made his senior debut for Galway.

I was only nineteen, and one week-day evening I went down to play a challenge match against Tipperary. Galway were short of players and it was a real baptism of fire. Those Tipperary lads were very tough! It was two years before I played for the seniors again, in Wembley against Derry.

An injury delayed his opportunity to stake a claim for a regular place on the team. He was a sub on the side that lost the Connacht semi-final to Roscommon in 1972, but the following year he became a regular on the team that marched triumphantly through the Connacht championship. Expectations across the county side were heightened further when Galway accounted for an Offaly side seeking three All-Irelands in a row. Then came the final against Cork.

Johnny Hughes after winning his first All-Star.

I was in my prime and my lifetime's ambition to play in an All-Ireland had been realised. We had a blow going into the match when we lost our star forward, Johnny Tobin. Nineteen-year-old Morgan Hughes came in for him, and handled the pressure very well. We scored 2–13 but we lost the All-Ireland by seven points. Jimmy Barry-Murphy and Jimmy Barrett caused us untold trouble.

I have no cribs about losing in 1973 because we were comprehensively beaten. We couldn't match their firepower. I wasn't too downbeat after it. I felt we had a good team and had the ability to win two or three All-Irelands later.

Hughes, and other Galway players, had youth on their side, after all.

After the All-Ireland we were staying in the Grand Hotel. A few of us, like 'Boxcar Willie', which was our nickname for Billy Joyce because he always led the singing, had girlfriends, but we had a very strict porter in our hotel and there was no way he was letting any of us bring girls up to our rooms. We discovered a plank of timber down in the basement, though, and we got the women in by getting them to walk up the plank and in through the windows.

The following year, Galway were back in the All-Ireland final against Dublin, having easily seen off Donegal in the semi-final.

Johnny Tobin had an outstanding game in the semi-final, scoring almost at will. You are better off, though, if you have a set of forwards who can score two or three points each, rather than being over-dependent on one player. If he is tied down you are in big trouble, as we discovered in the 1974 final when Johnny was held to a point. We had at least seventy-five per cent of the possession, but it came back to the same old story: lack of firepower up front. I got my second point with nine minutes to go to tie the match, but Jimmy Keaveney got a point from the kick-out and then another one and they beat us by five points in the end.

The key incident in the match was when Liam Salmon, who had never missed a penalty for Galway, had his spot-kick saved by Paddy Cullen.

I don't regard Liam's penalty as our worst miss, although if it had gone in we'd probably have won. In that game we had forwards who were kicking the ball straight at Paddy Cullen when he was lying on the ground. Throughout the match we missed chances that were easier to score. I was very disappointed that we lost that game. I was still young and never imagined that I would have to wait another nine years to play in an All-Ireland.

Some consolation for Hughes came when his club, Mountbellew, won the Galway Senior Football Championship that year. This meant that he would captain his county the following year. Things did not go to plan, however, in the Connacht championship.

I was really looking forward to the campaign in 1975 because I was captain. At that stage there was a lot of concern in Galway about our forwards. Pat Donnellan was playing well at club level and was drafted in for our first championship match against Sligo. He hadn't been in our first twenty-two and was wearing the number 24 jersey. I still recall the comment in the paper the next day: 'Pat Donnellan appeared on the scene wearing a faded jersey and the jersey, no more than the man, belonged to another decade.' Mickey Kearins beat us on his own that day. Anything he got inside the fifty-yard line went over the bar. He was like radar. It was very disappointing to go out so early.

1976 saw the Nestor Cup back in Galway, but Dublin beat them narrowly in the All-Ireland semi-final. Once again, it was a game Galway could have won.

The rest of the seventies was a bleak decade for Galway as Roscommon racked up four consecutive Connacht titles. But in 1981 Galway were back in the big time, beating Roscommon again to win the National League final, despite playing much of the match with only fourteen men after Stephen Joyce was sent off. It was a win against the odds, in more ways than one.

Around this time we had a bit of problem with our management. Liam O'Neill was put in charge of us, and he wanted to pick his own two or three selectors, which would have been the sensible thing to. In 1973, the year of my first All-Ireland, although John Dunne was our

*trainer, we had the crazy situation of having twelve or fourteen selectors
— you could have made a team out of them. Liam O'Neill stuck to his
guns, and when common sense did not prevail, he stood down. Mattie
McDonagh took over and brought us to victory in the league final.*

In the championship, however, Galway lost to Mayo, and a serious
injury in a club match consigned Hughes to the sidelines for a year.

*I was thirty-one when I had my injury. I had a bone taken from under
my knee and a plate and five screws inserted. A lot of people thought I
would never come back.*

He returned to the fold when coming on as a substitute against
Offaly in the 1982 All-Ireland semi-final. 'That semi-final was a
game we should have won,' he recalls ruefully.

*It was the story of my footballing life. We lost by a point, having
missed so many frees it was untrue. What was worse was that Offaly
went on to stop Kerry from winning the five-in-a-row.*

If he had thought 1982 was disappointing, it paled into
insignificance when compared with the disaster that lay around the
corner in 1983.

*I had come back from a serious injury and got myself into the best
shape of my life. I was absolutely flying at that stage. Then, in the All-
Ireland semi-final against Donegal, I remember turning quickly for
the ball and getting a twinge in the groin. I felt sore immediately after
the match. The next morning I couldn't get out of bed.*

*I trained very little before the All-Ireland, but I kept the scale of my
injury a secret from the media and from Mattie McDonagh. The
morning of the All-Ireland I walked to Mass from the hotel. I was
walking on the edge of the footpath when my foot slipped over the edge.
It was like a knife had been stuck in my leg and torn away the side. I
went back to the hotel after Mass and as I lay on my bed I said to
myself, 'You fool. Don't you dare go out and play in this match.' But
another voice was saying in my head, 'You've been playing for thirteen
years and this is Galway's year: we're going to win the All-Ireland.' I
let the heart rule the head, and decided to play.*

*The game wasn't long on before I could feel the leg going. Because
of the injury I was unable to make a quick turn and had to turn in a*

semi-circle. At one stage I made a foray up the field, and as I went to
kick the ball it was like someone cut a lump out of my leg. I had to go
off with about fifteen or twenty minutes to go.

Early in the game we were playing well, against the wind. I could
see that the Dublin forwards were a bit worried, and I told our
goalkeeper, Padraig Coyne, to take his time with the kick-outs. If he
could waste two or three minutes in the first half when we were against
the wind, then all the better for us. It was inexperience on Padraig's
part that he took the infamous quick kick-out which fell short to
Barney Rock, who lobbed the ball into our net. We were struggling
and it was certainly backs to the wall after that, but we were still in the
game. We had so many chances. You'd nearly have to compliment our
forwards; they were kicking spectacular wides when it seemed much,
much easier to score!

I have agonised about my decision to play in that game. I've often
thought that if I hadn't started in that game and came on for the last
twenty minutes, maybe in the forwards, we might have won that
game. I would at least have been able to punch the ball over the bar.

It was the closest I ever got to seeing a dressing-room turn into a
morgue. I was sick, sore and sorry; really, really sore and sorry. It was
my last game for Galway and a nightmare way to finish. Some people
only get one chance to win an All-Ireland. We got three and blew them
all, but that last one was just such a heartbreak.

And had I not played in the final I might have been able to play
again for Galway the following year — that is, if I had wanted to play
for another year. In fact, it was felt that I might never walk properly
again. It was two-and-a-half years before I played football again, and I
had the pleasure of finishing my career by winning another county title
with Mountbellew.

The 1983 final itself was overshadowed by a series of ugly
incidents which led to three players from Dublin and one from
Galway being sent off. Why did the game turn so nasty?

I remember a fairly hefty challenge from one of our players on one of
the Dublin lads. Tomás Tierney was sent off, but it should have been
that other player. Tomás was playing very well and it was a big blow
for us. Ciaran Duff was sent off for apparently kicking one of our lads

*on the ground, but I think that incident looked much worse than it
was. There was no real contact made.*

What then about the infamous tunnel incident said to have
involved Brian Mullins and Brian Talty at the interval?

*In those situations players get very hyped up and things happen that
normally wouldn't happen. Having said that, I honestly don't know
what happened. I didn't see anything, and I never asked anyone what
happened because I never wanted to know. From the moment the final
whistle went, for the last seventeen years, I have done everything I can
to forget everything about that game. It's the one match of my career
I've hardly ever spoken to anyone about, until now. It's the only one of
my All-Ireland final appearances I have on video, but I've never
watched it. I can never see myself going through that nightmare again.*

Fortunately, Hughes has happier memories of his time with
Galway to reflect on. A warm, affable man, the most revealing
insight into Johnny's personality is that the only photo of his
career evident in his home is almost completely hidden by the
stereo. The trophies most prominently displayed are not his two
All-Star awards (1974 and 1976), nor his two awards for Galway
Footballer of the Year (1974 and 1980), but his three daughters'
trophies for athletics and camogie.

When his inter-county career finished, Hughes found a new
outlet for his skills through his involvement in charity matches
with the Jimmy Magee All-Stars. He is fond of recalling the fun
and friendship of his footballing years. 'When we were training in
Tuam, there would always be fellas looking for shampoo
afterwards,' he reminisces.

*I always had shampoo, but Tomás Tierney and Tommy Joe Gilmore
were always swiping some off me.*

*I was working for a chemical company which manufactured a light
oil which looked like Clinic shampoo, and I poured some of this into
an empty bottle of shampoo which I left outside my shower in the
dressing-room. A few moments later I saw Tierney's foot coming over
and taking the bottle of shampoo, but I didn't let on to see him. He
rubbed it into his hair and passed it on to Tommy Joe. A few minutes*

later all hell broke loose. I can tell you it stopped them from stealing my shampoo for a long time after that.'

Who was the greatest character he came across?

Frank McGuigan was my most difficult opponent. He was both very strong and very skilful, and he could take you to the cleaners. He was also the best character I ever came across. We went on an All-Stars trip together. I was the captain of the team, and I remember knocking on Frank's door after he'd been out on the town all night, wondering would he be able to get up after only an hour-and-a-half's sleep. He got up and destroyed Brian Mullins in the Dublin midfield and was head and shoulders above any other player on the day.

One other name looms large in his discussion of great players: Roscommon's Dermot Earley.

I had many a great tussle with Dermot Earley. I remember drawing on a ball in the 1977 Connacht final but making contact with his hand and almost taking the tops off his four fingers. His reaction was to get his hand patched up and play one of the games of his life, and it had no effect on our friendship. He was very sporting, but he was tough: I remember him leaving me on the flat of my back another day. That's the way the game should be played, everybody giving their maximum. I never minded anybody trying to go through me. The only thing I hated was off-the-ball stuff, which I consider very cowardly.

I often said if there had been a transfer system in Gaelic football and we could get just one of either Dermot, Tony McManus or Mickey Kearins, we would have won three All-Irelands. All three would have stood out in any company. Connacht probably produced more great backs, like Harry Keegan, than great forwards in my time.

Galway's All-Ireland triumph in 1998 was a source of great pride to Hughes.

Obviously, the team I want to be most successful is Galway. However, if Galway are to lose, I want all the other Connacht counties to be successful. We've been the whipping boys for far too long, so I hope Galway's success in 1998 will inspire the other teams west of the Shannon. I felt when Galway won, they hadn't just won for themselves, but they had won for Dermot Earley, Harry Keegan, Mickey Kearins, Packy McGarty and all of us in Connacht who had soldiered for years but never won an All-Ireland medal.

History has forged a peculiarly close bond between these five counties, though the solidarity off the field is only matched by the intense rivalry between the counties on it. Hughes was to get a loud reminder of it in 1999.

I went to the replay of the FBD League final in Tuam with Mattie McDonagh. There were two fellas from Roscommon behind us and all through the match they kept shouting into our ears about how wonderful Roscommon were. After the match was over and Galway were beaten, I turned around to Mattie. The two lads were silent for a minute because they wanted to hear what I said. My comment was, 'In all fairness to Roscommon, they always were a great winter team.' The two boys were absolutely disgusted!

All through my career the rivalry between ourselves and Roscommon was great. They were the one team in Connacht we were always worried about playing. They had a great team in the late seventies and should have beat Kerry in the All-Ireland in 1980. The only problem they had was a lack of firepower.

In keeping with the inspiration underlying this book, Johnny selected a dream team of his greatest players from his era never to win an All-Ireland medal; however, he deliberately excluded Galway players.

Brian McAlinden (Armagh)
Harry Keegan (Roscommon) Gerry McCarville (Monaghan) Gabriel Kelly (Cavan)
Ger Feeney (Mayo) Paddy Moriarty (Armagh) Danny Murray (Roscommon)
Dermot Earley (Roscommon) Willie Joe Padden (Mayo)
Peter McGinnity (Fermanagh) Frank McGuigan (Tyrone) Mickey Kearins (Sligo)
Tony McManus (Roscommon) Eugene McKenna (Tyrone) Nudie Hughes (Monaghan)

NUDIE

One test of fame is when you are known simply by your first name: Bono, Gay, Packie; no further introduction required. In Gaelic football circles the name 'Nudie' is recognised instantly as that of Monaghan's most famous footballer, Eugene 'Nudie' Hughes, who helped Monaghan to three Ulster Senior Football Championships in 1979, 1985 and 1988.

'One of my family couldn't pronounce Eugene right,' Nudie explains his unique name, 'and I have never known myself to be called anything but 'Nudie' from the age of five or six.'

He was born into a big family in Castleblaney, home to legendary country-and-western singers Big Tom and Paddy Cole. He was certainly not born with a silver spoon.

'Twas tough. There were fourteen of us in the family — seven boys and seven girls — and there were only two bedrooms in the house. When I was nine years of age I was earning four quid a week for peeling spuds after

Nudie Hughes seeks possession.

school at the back of a chip-shop. My poor father, God rest him, hadn't it easy, and things were tight for all of us. I left school at the age of fifteen.

I started playing football in street leagues when I was about eight. When we finished school, we used to play in the commons, and in the summer time we played nearly up to midnight. One of the gang was 'Gunner' Brady, son of the famous 'Gunner' from Cavan.

When I was eighteen I started playing senior football for Castleblaney Faughs; that was back in 1975. It was the start of a great career for me, as I went on to win seven Monaghan Senior Football Championships and two Ulster senior football titles, in 1986 against Burren and in 1991 against Killybegs. I first played senior championship football against Tyrone in 1975 in the right half-back position. I was marking Brendan Donnelly. They won well that day.

Though his debut was not auspicious, Nudie was determined to leave his mark on the football world with a campaign of assiduous training. Sweat is the lubricant of dreams.

I used to train non-stop, and would think nothing of training for an hour and a quarter at half-six in the morning, and training with the county that evening. I spent a lot of time playing ball with left and right foot from close range — out to thirty-five yards — and would never move until I had scored ten with each foot. I'd always start in the centre of the goals, on the fourteen-yard line, and go either side of the post ten yards, because after reading The Christy Ring Story *and listening to Sean O'Neill I discovered that if you get the close things right, the others will follow naturally. Nowadays I am heavily involved in coaching at under-age level in Castleblaney, and I always quote Sean O'Neill's advice: 'Do the simple things well.' That's why I really admire the Meath style, which is to get the ball in quickly into the danger area.*

Monaghan made a giant breakthrough in 1979, winning their first Ulster title in forty-one years, only to lose to Kerry in the All-Ireland semi-final by 5–14 to 0–7. Although the game was a disaster for Monaghan it went well for Nudie.

It was our first Ulster title in forty-one years and the euphoria afterwards went to our heads. In the semi-final we were completely overawed by our first appearance in Croke Park. We were up against one of the greatest teams of all time — though it should be said that Kerry had only to win one game and they were in the All-Ireland semi-final; to win an Ulster title you had to win four matches. As they had a big pool to pick from, they could afford to rest players for the winter, whereas counties like Monaghan had to go flat-out to try and make the League play-offs to get some money for the county board. I think it's interesting that there were only two players from that Kerry side on the team of the millennium. That said, they played some wonderful football.

The semi-final went badly wrong for us, but everything went right for me that day. I was only twenty-one then and I had played well in the Ulster final, but that game gave me a national profile, especially as people remembered my name. At one stage in his commentary Mícheál O'Hehir said, 'And here comes Nudie Hughes for Nudie reason.'

That year, I became the first Monaghan player to win an All-Star. I'll never forget going to the airport and standing back near a pier with my two suitcases, but Tony Hanahoe came over to me and brought me up to the bar, where I found myself having a drink with the biggest names in football.

Much of the credit for the upturn in Monaghan's fortunes must go to their coach, Sean McCague, current president of the GAA. In the pre-McCague era, players from rival clubs wouldn't pass the ball to each other when they lined out for the county side. Monaghan's tough brand of football was captured in an old joke, that a late tackle in Monaghan was one that came the day after a match! McCague brought the county onto a different level.

Sean was a devoted and committed man. His commitment inspired great commitment from the players, and everything he asked of them he got. In terms of football style, his secret was to get to the ball first.

Monaghan's under-21 side, winners of the Ulster under-21 title in 1982, furnished new talent for the senior team, and two years later the county reached the semi-final of the National League, a match they lost to Meath. They lost to the same opposition in the Centenary Cup. Despite the defeats, Nudie greatly enjoyed the fellowship of the Meath team.

One night we drew with Meath in the Susan McCann Cup in Castleblaney, and the whole visiting bus-load stayed in the pub until half-three in the morning. We agreed to repeat the dose in the event of another draw. Meath beat us, as it turned out, but we had another session all the same.

In 1985, Monaghan made the breakthrough onto the national stage when they won their first National League title by beating Armagh 1–11 to 0–9.

For a full week we were treated as kings. Then it was down to serious training and, as everybody knows, we won the Ulster title again and then qualified for that famous All-Ireland semi-final against Kerry.

Both All-Ireland football semi-finals ended in draws that year. Dublin struggled in their match against Mayo, a game most often remembered for the fact that Mayo half-back John Finn sustained a broken jaw in an off-the-ball 'challenge'. Kerry appeared to have won the game against Monaghan when Mike Sheehy sent a free over the bar with time almost up, but one headlong assault saw Monaghan winning a free at midfield, and Eamonn McEneaney faced up to the last kick of the game and from fifty-five yards out calmly stroked the ball over the bar to tie the match: Kerry 1–12, Monaghan 2–9. Nudie shakes his head as he recalls that game.

We were flying, leading by five points coming up to half-time, and then John Kennedy hit a ball in from the wing very high and it hit the very tip of one of the posts and fell straight into Ger Power's hands, and he stuck it in the net from ten yards out. If you were to hit 10,000 balls in that direction, it would never come off the post exactly like that again. We went in at the break only two points ahead, which was a totally unfair reflection of our dominance. We were one of the unluckiest teams not to play in an All-Ireland final.

Like Roscommon in 1980, Monaghan were in the right place at the wrong time — when Kerry were in their prime. Had either of those teams been around in the 1990s they would almost certainly have won at least one All-Ireland. Nudie finally won an All-Ireland medal in 1998, at Masters level.

Although Nudie won an All-Star as a corner-back and two as a corner-forward (in the process becoming the first Ulster player to win three All-Stars), and won Railway Cup medals as a right corner-back, right half-back and a right corner-forward, and captained Ulster in 1986 as a right half-forward, none of these were in fact his favourite position. 'I preferred centre half-back to anything,' he says. 'You have to be a stopper and a creator.'

Who was the greatest character he met on the playing field?

John Egan. We were playing a Railway Cup match against Munster and I was marking John, one of the best players of all time. He was very hard to shake off the ball. We were standing talking — because I always talked to opponents, even though you would be told not to — and at one point he said, 'What's that man writing down on that piece of paper? He's a right looking eejit, isn't he?' As I turned to answer, John was sticking the ball into the net. I just shook my head and said, 'John, that's the last time I'll ever speak to you in a match.'

I used that same trick on Damien O'Reilly in 1988 when I was marking him in the Ulster final. At one stage in the game I said, 'Jaysus, there's an awful lot of people up on the hill. How many people would you say is up there?' As he looked up to make his guess the ball came in between us and I caught it without any obstruction and stuck it over the bar. He was taken off me immediately!

Who was his most difficult opponent? 'Dublin's Mick Kennedy. He was a very underrated player.'

He selected a club game when asked about his best match.

It would have to be the county final of 1985 or the county semi-final of 1986. Both were against our old rivals, Scotstown. We were badly handicapped in 1985 without Eamonn McEneaney, and we were missing Declan Loughman because of a broken leg. We lost that match by four points. I scored five points from centre-back, three with the right and two with the left. We won in 1986, and although I didn't score as much, the Argus newspaper said it was my finest hour.

At county level, in 1988 I was chosen as man of the match in the Ulster final against Tyrone. It was one of those days that everything went right, and I scored 1–3.

Nudie also made his mark on foreign shores.

We played in England one time, and our club game with Round Towers in New Eltham was cancelled. These boys came up from Bristol and got a few of us to play against Gloucester in a league final, totally illegally. I was the last brought on and about to hand my name, 'Brian Murphy', to the referee when the official from Bristol called me back and said, 'I'd better change that, as the other two I sent in were Brian Murphys and the ref would surely spot it.' We changed it to Aidan something or other, and went on to win the match.

That was by no means the most bizarre incident that occurred in Nudie's career.

We were playing against Clare in a league match in Ennis when some young fellas started throwing stones at our goalie, Bubbles McNeill. True to form, Bubbles started throwing stones back at them. The only problem was that he got so caught up with the stones, he completely forgot about the match, and when a Clare forward pumped a hopeful ball in from midfield, it went into the empty net. We lost the match by a point!

Nudie went to the Ulster team in centenary year to select his dream team:

Brian McAlinden (Armagh)

Joey Donnelly (Armagh) Gerry McGarville (Monaghan) Tony Scullion (Derry)

Ciaran Murray (Monaghan) Paddy Moriarty (Armagh) Jim Reilly (Cavan)

Joe Kernan (Armagh) Brian McGilligan (Derry)

Greg Blaney (Down) Eugene McKenna (Tyrone) Peter McGinnity (Fermanagh)

Martin McHugh (Donegal) Frank McGuigan (Tyrone) Nudie Hughes (Monaghan)

KEEPING UP WITH JONES

Mícheál Ó Muircheartaigh paints word-pictures like an artist. When he talks about football or hurling he always seems simply to hit the right note. The voice of Gaelic games, I put the question to him: who was the greatest player of them all?

That's too hard a question. I will say, though, that the best display I ever saw was by Galway's Sean Purcell. Most people remember him as a great Galway forward and for his association with Frankie Stockwell. Mayo had the best full-forward of the time, some would say of all time, Tom Langan, and Galway pulled off a shock move by bringing Sean back to mark him; that was when he gave the finest performance I ever saw. I saw him later that year in the All-Ireland semi-final against Kerry and again he was outstanding. Kerry were

winning well, but late in the game Galway moved him to midfield and he almost swung it for them. He had such skill and style that you could play him anywhere.

You have to remember that Gaelic football is completely different now. If it was possible to watch the great games of the 1920s, I'm sure we'd be dazzled by their spectacular high-fielding and kicking, but now football is a passing game — five passes for every kick. The other change is that the scores in games

The late, great Iggy Jones.

are much higher. If you look back at the All-Ireland finals in the 1930s, you might find a score like five points to four. Of course the answer that old-timers would give is that the backs were good in those times as well: I let you work out the implication for yourself!

Players are much fitter and more mobile, too — you could never imagine a player like Pat Spillane staying in the one position. But when the famous Dr Eamon O'Sullivan trained Kerry, on and off, from the 1920s to the 1960s, he was a firm believer in all players keeping to their positions. He actually wrote a book about his ideas — I think the name of it was The Art and Science of Gaelic Football *— and he pointed out that, for Gaelic football to be seen at its very best, every tussle for the ball should be between just two players. He also said that good kicking and fielding would win out in the end. He took it to an extreme, but he did win a lot of All-Irelands with Kerry. His theory would be perfect if every player was the ideal and perfect player, but of course they're not. It's now a running and supporting game, as they say.*

Who, then, was the greatest never to win an All-Ireland medal?

God, you could make a team of them! In hurling, generations of great Wexford players went without winning an All-Ireland. A lot of great Galway hurlers, like Josie Gallagher and Seanie Duggan, never won one, and if you like they laid the foundations for modern-day hurling in Galway. Josie Gallagher was as good a hurler as I ever saw. In football there's Gerry O'Reilly, Jim Rogers and Andy Phillips of Wicklow, and if you go west you have the great Gerry O'Malley of Roscommon and of course Dermot Earley, who played so well for so long with Roscommon. If you moved north, you would have T.P. Treacy of Fermanagh and Iggy Jones of Tyrone.

The late Iggy Jones of Tyrone was one of the great personalities of Gaelic football in the 1940s and '50s. Iggy first came to prominence on the national stage in the inaugural All-Ireland Colleges final in 1946, when his three goals helped St Patrick's College, Armagh, fight back to snatch the title away from St Jarlath's College, Tuam. The Northerners, who also had Eddie and Jim Devlin in the team, trailed at half-time by 2–3 to 0–6. Jones had scored four points in the first half, and in the second he added three goals, the highlight of which came from a solo run when he spread the entire St Jarlath's defence before unleashing a rocket of a shot to the Tuam net.

The Galway side were powered by the great Sean Purcell, and the following year his domination in the Colleges final helped reverse the result. By that stage, Iggy had left school and was too old to play on the Tyrone minor team that won the Ulster minor championship in 1946. He had already played on the Tyrone senior team for two years. Strangely, his ambition was not to win a regular place for Tyrone but to play at senior level for his club, Dungannon Tomás Ó Cléirigh. In the course of a radio interview in 1992 he said,

I always felt there was no higher ambition than to play for my club. When I did wear the county jersey I would have died for it, even though we won very few matches in the early years. I find it very strange today when I hear about players who have to be motivated before playing games. To me just pulling on either my club or county jersey was all the motivation I needed.

Iggy's introduction to championship football was not the happiest.

My championship debut was against Down. The first time I got the ball I passed it to a team-mate and raced on to take the return pass, but instead he booted the ball two miles in the air! I knew that I was not going to have a big influence on that match.

Success in football comes in cycles. When he was president of the GAA, Jack Boothman went to the funeral of the legendary Paddy Bawn Brosnan at a time when Kerry football was in the doldrums. He went to meet the funeral at the graveyard, and while he waited for the cortège to arrive one of the gravediggers pointed out to him the graves of all the famous footballers. 'It's a very impressive collection. Isn't it?' the gravedigger said to Boothman.

'It is indeed,' the GAA president replied, 'but the way things are going at the moment, you'll have to dig them up again if Kerry are ever going to win anything!'

Iggy Jones came on to the scene when Cavan was the super-power in Gaelic football. Cavan's success left Jones with mixed feelings.

*You could say I was a half Cavan man because my father was from
there. When an Ulster team goes to Croke Park the neutral Ulster fans
will always back the team from their province, and if Tyrone weren't
doing well we supported Cavan. The only problem I had with Cavan's
success was that they completely dominated the Ulster team, and they
were a very clannish bunch so that the rest of us never got much of a
look in. I would have been happier to have played with Ulster when
the great Down team came along because my game would have been
more suited to their style. The only thing was that when we finally
made the breakthrough in 1956 and won the Ulster final, we beat
Cavan. That really made the whole occasion for us.*

In the run-up to the Ulster final Tyrone stepped up their
preparations, doing an hour-and-a-half's training every night for
two weeks before the game. There were none of the facilities that
top-class players enjoy today: after training the players washed
themselves from a galvanised bucket on the sideline. After taking
the Ulster title, Tyrone narrowly lost the All-Ireland semi-final to
the eventual champions Galway. It was a match that Jones was
never allowed to forget.

*I had a goal chance to win the game when we were trailing by just two
points. I made a run and cut along the in-line. You don't score goals
from there so I looked for a team-mate to pass to, but there was no
Tyrone forward there for me. I remember cutting in from the in-line
and getting on to the edge of the small parallelogram. The Galway
goalie Jack Mangan was toward the near post. I thought to myself, 'I'll
not get it past him but I'll get it over him.' I punched the ball over his
head, but unfortunately Mangan got his hand to it. Thirty years later I
went to a school to speak to the children and this boy came up to me
and said, 'My Dad told me you were the man that lost the All-Ireland
for Tyrone!'*

The match brought Jones face to face once more with Sean
Purcell, whom he regarded as the greatest player of all time.
According to legend, after Galway won the All-Ireland in 1956,
Sean Purcell was waiting in Galway for the bus to Tuam, not
realising that the last bus had gone. However, a driver on his way
back to the garage with an empty bus spotted 'the Master', and

though it was against all regulations he stopped and told Purcell to hop in. Four miles out from Tuam the driver nearly had a stroke when he saw an inspector standing in the middle of the road waving him down. The inspector demanded an explanation. 'I have the Master here,' the driver answered meekly.

'You can't be serious!' said the inspector, boarding the bus to verify the fact. Then he turned to the driver again. 'Turn around and get back to the garage. How could you drive the Master in a single-decker bus? Get him a double-decker straight away so that he can go upstairs if he fancies a cigarette!'

Jones emigrated in 1956, but after Tyrone won the Ulster championship in 1957 he returned for the All-Ireland semi-final against Louth. He considered that match to be the biggest disappointment of his career.

There was a lot of discussion about whether I should play or not. I was fit but I wasn't match fit. In the end it was decided I should play. The line of reason was that I would at least stop Stephen White from coming up the field and scoring for Louth, as he had been doing all year. We felt Galway were the team to beat that year, and if we could beat them we would win the All-Ireland. Yet despite missing a first-half penalty, Louth won the match by six points, thanks in no small measure to the lethal boot of Kevin Beahan.

Our reign in Ulster didn't last the third year. We thought all we had to do against Down was turn up. Over-confidence beat us, as that Down side were a coming team and went on to win two All-Irelands.

Although Jones continued to play for a few more years, Tyrone had no further brush with glory in his playing days. Tyrone finally got to an All-Ireland final in 1986, only to lose to Kerry. Iggy Jones felt that their defeat could be attributed to just one reason: injury to Eugene McKenna.

When we were leading by seven points we needed Eugene to win a few big balls at midfield and steady the ship for us. If he had been fully fit he would have done that.

Throughout his playing career, Iggy Jones never weighed more than nine to nine-and-a-half stone. His speed of thought and foot kept him out of trouble. He would have loved to have played the game in modern times, as he believed that the speed of the modern game would have suited a player of his light physique. And he reckoned he would win twenty penalties in one of today's matches because of the way the rules are applied now.

Iggy offered a surprising perspective when asked about the reason why Tyrone did not win the All-Ireland in the late 1950s.

> *We should have put all our eggs into the one basket and devoted all our energies to winning it. The problem was that our officials were too honest. When we were invited to play in a tournament, no matter how unimportant, they insisted on putting out our strongest team because they thought people were entitled to see the very best. That was very noble, but we paid a high price in terms of wear and tear and injuries when we could have benefited from a rest.*
>
> *I remember one such tournament match when I had a bad clash of heads with Noel O'Reilly and the blood was pumping out of me. By any stretch of the imagination I should have gone off, especially considering there was nothing at stake. It would have been different if it was an All-Ireland or even an Ulster final. I needed stitches, but I didn't come off. One of our mentors came on and said to me, 'Look at our subs bench. Do you see any player there good enough to take your place?'*

Lethal Weapon

Micheál Kearins in full flight was a sight to make the blood tingle. Gaelic games commentator Mícheál Ó Muircheartaigh furnished the definitive epitaph to Kearins's career when he said, 'Some players are consistent; some players are brilliant; but Mícheál Kearins was consistently brilliant.'

As a boy his hero was the great Sligo full-back Nace O'Dowd. It was only after he completed his education, at Ballinaleg National School and St Muirdeach's College in Ballina, that he really made his mark in the footballing world. He first played for Sligo minors in 1960, losing out in the Connacht championship to a Galway side powered by Noel Tierney and Johnny Geraghty that went all the way to win the All-Ireland.

The following year he made his debut for the senior team against Cavan in a league game in Ballymote, and he played for the county at all three levels that year. In all, he played seventeen successive championship seasons with Sligo from 1962 to 1978. There were many disappointments, particularly losing the Connacht final to Galway in 1965, but as he himself says,

My dedication and love of Gaelic football always kept me going.

Mickey Kearins poses for the cameras.

His introduction to championship football in 1962 was the story of his career in shorthand: so near and yet so far. Sligo led by a point against the reigning champions, but Roscommon stole victory with a goal in the last kick of the game, and went on to contest the All-Ireland final.

Micheál's place in the lore of Gaelic football is secure if only for his phenomenal scoring feats, setting records that had no equivalent in the past and are never likely to find even an echo in the future. He was the country's leading marksman in competitive games in four different years: 1966, 1968, 1972 and 1973. In the drawn 1971 Connacht final he scored a record fourteen points, five from play and nine from placed balls. He won two Railway Cup medals in a thirteen-year career with Connacht, in 1967 and 1969. Two years later he scored twelve points for Connacht against the Combined Universities in the Railway Cup, all from placed balls. With the Combined Universities leading by 3–9 to 0–17, Connacht got a line ball forty-five yards out in the dying seconds and Kearins slotted it over the bar to earn Connacht a replay.

Kearins was a natural rather than a manufactured talent. Although he ranks with stars like Ollie Campbell as among the greatest place-kickers in the history of Irish sport, he did very little actual practice in that area.

> *Especially in the early years I did a lot of physical training on my own — I would run a few miles early in the morning maybe four times a week. I never bothered practising my free-taking, not even taking a practice one in the kick-about before a match.*

The score which stands out in his memory is 'a sideline kick from thirty yards in the Connacht final of 1971 against Galway.'

All through his long career Kearins never shed the burden of having the weight of Sligo fans' expectations resting on his shoulders.

> *I was always nervous before a game, knowing Sligo were depending on me. To slot the first free over was always very important to help me to relax.*

He won an All-Star award in the inaugural year of 1971 at left half-forward, the first of only two Sligo men to win the award;

Barnes Murphy became the second in 1975. Kearins was also a replacement All-Star in 1972; indeed, a major controversy ensued when he was omitted from the original selection.

He won a magnificent seven football championships with his club, St Patrick's, Dromard, two at junior and five at senior level, and he won two senior county medals with Ballisodare. He also played in — and lost — three National League semi-finals with Sligo. He played in three Connacht senior football finals, losing to Galway in 1965 and 1971 before finally winning the title in 1975.

With a Cinderella county like Sligo it was inevitable that Kearins's career would be marked by the anguish of seeing his team lose often. His career was very much about being willing to accept long periods of frustration in return for one day of glory, like the once-in-a-lifetime ecstasy of winning the Connacht final. The fact that he scored thirteen points in the match helped to make the occasion all the more memorable for him. 'Winning the Connacht championship in 1975 was a great honour,' he says. Even so, it was not the highlight of his career.

Winning the senior county championship with St Patrick's, Dromard, in 1968 was the best moment of my career.

After his retirement from playing, Kearins became a referee. His career with the whistle is probably best remembered for the time he sent Meath star, Colm O'Rourke, off the pitch.

It was an incident after half-time and he got a heavy shoulder while in possession. It knocked the ball out of his hands, but he didn't try to retrieve it; instead he came after me. He followed me the whole way down the field, sharing 'pleasantries' with me! I had no option but to send him off.

The two had another heated exchange subsequently, in the 1988 All-Ireland semi-final, when Kearins was a linesman.

There was a line-ball incident and he felt I gave the wrong decision. I know now, having seen the replay on telly, that I was wrong and he was right. I would have to say, though, that he was a great player and made the Meath forward line tick while he was in his prime. He was their playmaker.

Kearins did not have to think too deeply when asked about his most difficult game to referee.

It was an All-Ireland semi-final between Cork and Dublin. I had to send Keith Barr off that day. He got involved in an incident five minutes earlier and he ran thirty or forty yards to get involved in that second incident. There was an awful lot of off-the-ball stuff that day and it's very hard to manage those games.

In fact the tension escalated to such an extent that Kearins pulled captains Dinny Allen and Gerry Hargan aside before the start of the second half and instructed them to warn their players about their behaviour. He did not get quite the response he hoped for from Allen who, when asked by the Cork lads about what the referee said, allegedly claimed Kearins had simply wished them well for the second half and hoped the awful weather would improve.

Sligo's most famous footballer rates Leitrim's Packy McGarty as the greatest player never to win an All-Ireland medal, and selects a fellow Connacht man when asked about the greatest player he ever saw.

It has to be Sean Purcell. He could play anywhere and had all the skills. Mick O'Connell's anticipation for fielding was great, too. My most difficult opponent, though, was Donegal's Brian McEniff.

He was, he says, 'greatly honoured' to be selected at left half-forward on the Team of the Century for players who never won an All-Ireland senior medal.

Though the pitch of his conversation is undramatic, almost downbeat, the depth and authenticity of his experience fills my mind with images of summer afternoons in Castlebar, or poorly attended league fixtures when the only sound of applause came from the rain rattling on the slats of the stand roof. Anyone interviewing him is unlikely to be offered a stream of cosy reminiscences, but there are one or two.

My first Railway Cup game was against Leinster in Ballinasloe. At the start, as I was moving into position before the ball was thrown in, I noticed my immediate opponent, Paddy McCormack, digging a strip along the ground with his boot.

He said, 'You're young Kearins, from Sligo. I presume you expect to go back to Sligo this evening?'

'Hopefully,' I replied.

'Don't pass that mark and you have a fair chance of getting there.'

I passed the mark a few times and played well on him, scoring four points from play, and I still travelled home to Sligo safe that evening!

Kearins's dream team is:

Johnny Geraghty (Galway)
Donie O'Sullivan (Kerry) Noel Tierney (Galway) Tom O'Hare (Down)
Páidí Ó Sé (Kerry) Gerry O'Malley (Roscommon) Martin Newell (Galway)
Mick O'Connell (Kerry) Jim McKeever (Derry)
Matt Connor (Offaly) Sean Purcell (Galway) Pat Spillane (Kerry)
Mike Sheehy (Kerry) Sean O'Neill (Down) Paddy Doherty (Down)

ELATION ONCE AGAIN

One of the many stories told about Christy Ring is that once, as he was leading the Cork team out of the dressing-room, he took off his jersey, held it up to his players, and asked them to look at the colour and think of what it meant to them. The team went out with fire in their bellies and played out of their skins.

One footballer who never needed any motivational ploys to be enthused by the Cork jersey was Kevin Kehilly. He first sprang to prominence as a seventeen-year-old in 1967, when he played for the Cork minors. The Cork Junior Championship medal which he should have won in the same year was postponed to the following March when the final, delayed by an outbreak of foot-and-mouth disease in Britain, was finally contested. In 1971 he won an intermediate championship medal courtesy of a victory over St Finbarr's, a team drawing on the emerging talent of Jimmy Barry-Murphy. Kehilly was a dual star also, and won a Fitzgibbon medal with UCD and two Cork senior hurling medals.

It was at football, though, that he won his two All-Star awards, in 1980 at full-back and in 1982 at right full-back. Like other players featured here, Kehilly's collection of medals is much smaller than it might have been because his career coincided with the golden era of Kerry football. How difficult was it for the lecturer in Cork Institute of Technology to keep going when the rebel county was losing the Munster final every year?

There were times when it was hard. It did get demoralising, but I would have to say that we never went into any of those Munster finals not thinking we were going to win. We never had an inferiority complex even though they beat us well a few times. We always enjoyed those matches, even though Mick O'Dwyer always hyped us up by saying Cork was the most difficult opposition he expected to meet all year. We always got on well with the Kerry lads. I played with most of them on the Munster team and I always felt they gave the Cork lads plenty of respect.

I suppose what kept us going was the enjoyment we got from playing. We were all passionately in love with the game. We had a lot of craic and fun. Although we had a lot of disappointments in the Munster championship, we at least had the consolation of getting to a league final in 1979, which we lost to Roscommon, and of beating Kerry in the League final the following year. It was a big thrill for me to win a national title at last.

An rud is annamh is iontach. People turn to sport for the impossible, the miraculous. On the field, David can sometimes topple Goliath. The magic of sporting competition was highlighted when Offaly beat Kerry to win the All-Ireland in 1982. The following year, the Kerry team, universally acknowledged as the greatest team of all time, was seeking an unprecedented nine Munster titles in a row. The match gave Kehilly the highlight of his career.

The game that stands out the most for me was the Munster final in 1983, when the long period of frustration at the hands of Kerry ended and we snatched the game in the last minute with Tadghie Murphy's goal. What I

Kevin Kehilly emerges with the ball in a League game against Dublin, with Cork corner-back Seamus O'Sullivan and Anton O'Toole in close attendance.

remember most about the day was going in to visit the late Tom Creedon in hospital with some of the rest of the players. There was horrific thunder and lightning as we were walking through the corridors of the hospital, and we wondered if the game would go ahead. In fact the weather turned out to be quite good in the afternoon.

Jack O'Shea was the Kerry captain that day, confident, as most people were, that Kerry would take another Munster title. Indeed Mícheál Ó Muircheartaigh, who was training the Kerry lads in Dublin at the time, also helped Jacko on his victory speech. And then, when Kerry lost the match, there was another twist to the story. Kerry, the holders, forgot to bring the Munster Cup with them to the final, and it was only quick thinking by Frank Murphy, the Cork secretary, that saved the day. He rummaged around and found a cup — apparently the Cork Junior Championship trophy — and that was presented to Cork captain Christy Ryan. Nobody seemed to notice; certainly the Cork players, with a fabulous victory under their belts, were not going to worry about the silverware.

If 1983 provided Kehilly with his greatest memory, it also provided him with his biggest disappointment.

Losing the All-Ireland semi-final replay to Dublin by such a big margin was a real downer, especially as we were playing in our own backyard.

Yet Kehilly was not allowed to get the defeat out of proportion.

I got a call afterwards from Ray Cummins and he told me that Tom Creedon had died. Tom and I were very close friends and our wives were very good friends too. Tom had been critically ill after an accident in his van, and his death was a tragic loss for his wife and young family. That really put sport in perspective.

Kehilly has noticed significant changes in the game since he retired.

The big difference is that the game is much faster now. As a back you are finished unless you have speed. The other change is that there is much less emphasis now on staying in your position. Backs turn up in the forwards and vice versa, but the single best change is the speed of the game. On the downside, I don't think you see as much high fielding in the game as you used to.

His selection as his most difficult opponent will come as no surprise to fans of the game. 'Eoin Liston,' he says immediately.

He came on so much from his early days. I played on him at the start of his career and there was no comparison with the player I marked then and the guy I marked a few years later. He was very imposing physically and yet he was surprisingly mobile. He was a great man to lay off a ball, which was bad news for any team playing Kerry because he had wonderful forwards to pass to wherever he looked. The only thing I will say about the Bomber, though, is that I found it much easier to mark him whenever Jack O'Shea wasn't playing. Jacko always gave him a wonderful service, and Eoin wasn't as dangerous when he wasn't getting perfect balls into him all the time.

I marked Jimmy Keaveney a few times. He was a very different player to the Bomber but you could never give him an inch because he would really do damage. He was deadly accurate.

If he was 'going to war' in a big match, which player would he most like to have in his corner?

Páidí Ó Sé. He was tough as teak and played as if his life depended on it. You'd always know he would never let you down, and when the going got tough he'd come up trumps for the team.

There is no hesitation either when he is asked who the best player he ever saw was.

Dermot Earley. I spent a year with him in Strawberry Hill College in London, doing a one year post-graduate course in physical education. Dermot was a wonderful player. He had so many facets to his game. He was an exceptional fielder, always controlled things very well in the middle of the field, always scored a lot and was deadly from frees. He had a perfectionist streak to him: he trained very hard and he looked after himself really well. He must rank as the greatest player never to win an All-Ireland medal. Gerry O'Malley was another great Roscommon player never to win an All-Ireland.

Throughout Kehilly's career, his Cork colleagues always kept him in laughs.

When I was finishing playing football, it was the era of the roving full-forward. I was the last of the traditional full-backs who marshalled the square, and it was a big culture shock for me to have to start running half-way out the field and running back in again for the whole match. It was tough on the body, and Billy Morgan was always winding me up before a match saying, 'Kevin, keep close to the goal today. I didn't bring any oxygen!'

Kevin's dream team of the men from his era is:

Paddy Cullen (Dublin)
Nudie Hughes (Monaghan) John O'Keeffe (Kerry) Robbie Kelleher (Dublin)
Páidí Ó Sé (Kerry) Paddy Moriarty (Armagh) Martin O'Connell (Meath)
Dermot Earley (Roscommon) Jack O'Shea (Kerry)
Anton O'Toole (Dublin) Kevin Kilmurray (Offaly) Pat Spillane (Kerry)
Mick Sheehy (Kerry) Eoin Liston (Kerry) Matt Connor (Offaly)

KING STEPHEN

Stephen King's exploits for Cavan have elevated him to the status of local hero, and left him a treasure chest of memories to look back on in his own self-effacing way.

Growing up in Killeshandra, the biggest influence on his career was Sergeant Peter Maguire, who nurtured his talents with the local club, Killeshandra Leaguers. He won a minor league, junior championship and three intermediate championships with them.

As a youngster he was always a precocious talent.

When I was fourteen I played under-16 for the county. When I was sixteen I played for the county minors, and when I was minor I played under-21 for the county. I played my first match for Cavan seniors when I was eighteen. It was against Meath in a challenge match in Kells, and I never really looked back after that.

For seventeen years King's career progressed without any success at inter-county level, though he had the consolation of winning four

Stephen preparing for the most momentous match of his life.

Railway Cup medals. 'The Railway Cup was hugely important to me, particularly in the 1980s,' he recalls.

At the time, Ulster football was in the doldrums, and the Railway Cup allowed us to rub shoulders with players from the great Kerry team and match ourselves with many of the greatest players of all time. Ulster, probably more so than the other provinces, always took the competition very seriously, and it paid off with the success we had.

Despite the disappointments he experienced with Cavan, his zest for the drama of the game was undiminished.

It probably wasn't as difficult as people might think to keep going. I got great enjoyment from playing and it was a great way of meeting people. Having said that, it was hard to lose Ulster championships year after year. You would ask yourself: Why am I doing this to myself? Then a few months later the League started, and after you won a couple of matches the hunger came back as strong as ever.

The length of his career saw him play under a number of different managers, and though he admired them all, one stood out.

I would have to say they were all very good. People like Gabriel Kelly and P.J. Carroll were very committed; Eugene McGee came with a big reputation, having won an All-Ireland with Offaly, and he certainly was a very deep thinker about the game. But Martin McHugh was definitely the best of them all. He was the first to really adapt our style of football to the modern era and really move us up with the times, taking us away from a catch-and-kick style to a faster style of play.

In Martin's first year in charge we got to the Ulster final. We could have won it but we were too naive on the day. In 1997 we were a more mature outfit, and for a few players like me it was the end of the line, so it was do or die. We got out of jail to snatch a draw with Fermanagh and I think we knew then that it was going to be our year.

Cavan's victory in the Ulster final that year prompted celebrations the likes of which had not been seen in the county since the glory days of John Joe O'Reilly. The local media celebrated the win as the major news story of the year.

Everyone in Cavan went haywire. I'll never forget the scene in Clones after we won. You couldn't see a blade of grass on the pitch because of the sea of blue and white.

But if their Championship win provided Stephen with the highlight of his career,

definitely the low point was losing the All-Ireland semi-final to Kerry. As a team we didn't perform to the best of our abilities on the day. We missed the boat. It was all the more galling because I still believe we would have won the All-Ireland that year had we beaten Kerry.

When asked about his favourite character in the game, he replies,

Anthony Molloy from Donegal. He's got such a great way with people and is so friendly. It's no wonder he's such a popular guy.

He is equally emphatic about the greatest players he ever saw.

Jack O'Shea and Brian Mullins. They would have made a fantastic and unbeatable combination if they had played for the same team.

A clean player, Stephen King has strong views on one of the less savoury aspects of football today.

The GAA has had a lot of controversies in recent years with violent incidents on the pitch, and they must do something about it. Probably the most worrying thing is that some of these incidents have taken place in under-age and college matches. I have no time for the off-the-ball stuff that's spoiling the game. We have to face up to some hard choices if we are to stamp this out.

I also feel that we have to take a long, hard look at the rules of the game. I think football is being killed by the stop-start way in which matches are being played. It's ruining the game because the pace is so slow now. When you contrast it with the speed of hurling, football is playing catch-up.

Having climbed the mountain in 1997, Cavan football went into something of a decline afterwards. King sees it more as a transition than a crisis.

The change of management probably had something to do with it. Then there were players like myself who stepped down, so a new panel had to be developed.

'It takes time for things to settle,' he says philosophically.

Major controversy erupted when Martin McHugh's successor, Liam Austin, was forced to resign as Cavan manager because of 'player-power'. King subsequently became the punters' favourite but he declined to go forward for the post.

I had just started up my own pub in Killeshandra so there was no way I could even consider taking the position. I would love, though, to get the job some time in the future.

How does King feel about 'player-power'?

In general I think it's a bad thing. The one thing I would say, though, is that players should be properly looked after by the GAA, because it's the players that generate the crowds and the revenue. Once that happens, I think players should concentrate on playing and not get involved in politics, if that's what you want to call it.

One of the highlights of King's career was playing for Ireland in the Compromise Rules against Australia.

It was a huge honour to play for my country. Eugene McGee was in charge in the squad and we did a huge amount of training. It was a tremendous experience and a great outlet for amateur players. I think it has a good future and should be encouraged.

The series offered him one of the most bizarre sights of his career.

We were coming off the pitch and one of my opponents was chastising me and giving me fierce abuse. To be honest, it didn't really bother me, but Brian McGilligan was coming up behind me and he wasn't very impressed. He came up and knocked out your man's gum-shield and stamped on it with his foot. I've never seen anybody shut up so fast!

Stephen's dream team is:

Billy Morgan (Cork)
Robbie O'Malley (Meath) Mick Lyons (Meath) Tony Scullion (Derry)
Páidí Ó Sé (Kerry) Paddy Moriarty (Armagh) Jim Reilly (Cavan)
Jack O'Shea (Kerry) Brian Mullins (Dublin)
Martin McHugh (Donegal) Greg Blaney (Down) Matt Connor (Offaly)
Peter Canavan (Tyrone) Colm O'Rourke (Meath) John Egan (Kerry)

Amongst Lilywhites

Pat Mangan played for Kildare senior football team from 1964 to 1979 without ever being dropped for a match. In 1972 he was Sports Star of the Week in the *Irish Independent* on foot of his commanding display at centre half-back against Mattie Kerrigan of Meath in the Leinster semi-final. Yet, although he travelled as a replacement All-Star to San Francisco in 1973, he never actually won the award. That a player of his class should be so overlooked is a damning example of a player who loses out because his county fails to do well in the championship.

Mangan made his senior county debut against Wicklow in Aughrim in 1964, becoming one of an elite group to play minor and senior county football in the same year. Curiously, he was only a substitute on the under-21 side that year. The following year he announced his arrival on the centre stage with his performances for the Kildare senior team, though they lost to Meath in the Leinster semi-final. He also starred in the under-21 team which beat Offaly in a thrilling display of football, saw off a star-studded Down side in their own backyard, and then made history in an epic All-Ireland final against Cork, when they won Kildare's first All-Ireland title since 1928.

We started out in February of that year and nobody had much hope for us. We played Meath in the first round and beat them in Maynooth. The Offaly team we beat in the Leinster final were hot favourites. There was a tremendous buzz in Kildare coming up to the All-Ireland after we beat Down. We had an exceptional team, and I remember people like Mícheál Ó Muircheartaigh saying that it was one of the best games ever played in Croke Park. It was a very tight match but we pulled away in the last ten minutes. I remember thinking to myself: this is tremendous. It seemed inevitable that with normal progress this team would go on to win a senior All-Ireland.

The following year we were red-hot favourites to retain our title. We had twelve of the team that had won the previous year and we waltzed through Leinster without being put under any pressure. We beat a very good Kerry team in Newbridge to win the semi-final and we were unbackable favourites to win the final against Roscommon. They had not had an impressive semi-final performance, and the scribes and obviously a lot of Kildare players thought it was going to be one-way traffic. However, dedication and commitment was lacking, and we got caught on the hop.

We had struggled for periods in a number of matches during the campaign, but once we turned it on we blew the opposition out of the water. In the second half of the All-Ireland we stepped up a gear and moved about five points clear of Roscommon. We looked to be coasting home, but when Roscommon moved Dermot Earley to midfield he pumped in a few great balls to the forwards and Roscommon got two goals from them. Roscommon went a point up with about a minute to go. Kildare got the ball from the kick-out. I remember Pat Dunney cutting in from the left-hand side and going for goal, but his shot was blocked down. He thought we were two points down; I've no doubt if he knew the score he would have taken the point and the game would have been a draw, and we would have won the replay.

It was a terrible blow to Kildare football, particularly after we had been beaten that year in the seniors by a very experienced Meath team — our team was powered by the under-21 side, and were very young. In that game,

Pat Mangan and Christy O'Connor Jr. share an awarding moment.

*Meath took the initiative in the first half but we really got going in the
second half and were coming hard at them. Then came what in my
opinion was the most controversial incident in my time with Kildare.*

*With what we thought was a minute to go, and trailing by a point,
we got a free about sixty yards out from the goal at the Canal End. Jack
Donnelly came out to take the kick, though it was too far out for him
to score. As the free dropped on the fourteen, Jimmy Cummins caught
the ball, turned and was about to shoot when he was buried in the
ground. We were delighted; we thought it was going to be a fourteen-
yards free and Donnelly would tap it over the bar for the equaliser.
Then the referee, John Dowling, walked in, picked up the ball and blew
for full-time. It was a real hammer-blow, especially when combined
with the under-21 defeat.*

Mangan sees the effect of the defeats as a watershed in the
football fortunes of the county. Panic measures were taken to
alleviate the crisis, and had the opposite effect to that intended.

*It sparked a lot of changes in the selectors and they in turn chopped and
changed the players. People said some of the young lads were not
mature enough to win, so some of the old guys were brought back.
Even though we had the basis of a very good team — and I played in
five more senior Leinster finals — we never really seemed to get it
together after that. The players' confidence seemed to wane and their
commitment dipped also. The turn-out at sessions was pathetic. It was
no wonder we won nothing.*

A spell as player–manager of the county side gave Mangan a
greater insight into the shortcomings of the team.

*I did a year as trainer of Kildare in 1972–73. Every year we had a
different one; we had more trainers than Sheik Mohammed! It was a
difficult task, especially as I found myself doing tasks the county
secretary should have been doing, organising matches and pitches and
so on. I put a lot of effort into it and got on well with the players, but
it put a big strain on me and my own performance and I stood down
after we lost to Offaly in the Leinster semi-final. It could have been a
different story if we had a good settled team and things were going
well, but we had difficulties with some players coming training. Even*

though I would have come up the ranks with them, I didn't get the response I needed.

While Mangan feels that Kildare were the architects of their own downfall, he acknowledges that other factors contributed to their failure to make the breakthrough.

Leinster is a very difficult province to win. We were also unfortunate enough to come up against Offaly in the early 1970s, and just when we had started to get the measure of Offaly, along came Dublin in 1974. We beat them in a Division Two league final in early 1974, but Heffo did his homework and later that year reversed the result in the championship. They went on to become one of the best teams of the era; some of their matches against Kerry were classics, the best I ever saw. They played some very attractive football, but had players who were equally good at reducing the effectiveness of the opposition with questionable tactics.

Fate decreed that Mangan would retire without even a Leinster senior medal.

I gave up playing for Kildare in 1979 when I was thirty-three, after we lost to Meath following a replay in the second round of the Leinster championship. Having played for sixteen years and had all the disappointments in the meantime, it got very difficult to motivate myself.

In the League campaign the previous year I was moved into full-forward, and when that happens you know you're getting close to the sideline. In that campaign we played Kerry in Killarney when they were at their peak. I played on John O'Keeffe. I got the biggest runaround I ever got that day. The quality of the ball into me wasn't great, but whatever ball came, O'Keeffe cleaned me out.

Kerry got seven goals in that game and the following day a good friend of mine told me that he thought it was time for me to hang up my boots. I said no, I couldn't go out on that performance. I knew I had played dreadfully but, equally, that I was capable of better. I didn't know whether I'd get picked or not, but I declared myself available for the following match, against Cork in Newbridge. The game went well and I redeemed myself somewhat. That winter my head knew where I wanted to be but my legs just couldn't get me there. Your appetite for the game begins to go, particularly as your team doesn't show any signs of making the breakthrough. I had family at the time, and you say to yourself, what's the point?

Mangan was more fortunate at club level, winning seven senior championship medals with Carbury. And in 1998 he had the pleasure of seeing Kildare at last come in from the footballing wilderness. His analysis of the reasons for the team's breakthrough is very concise.

I think it's all down to one man: Mick O'Dwyer. He brought the organisation and the football skill that was lacking over the years. He's a very, very strong personality and the most positive guy that you could ever talk to.

He came to Kildare when they were at their lowest. Kildare people love their football and are great supporters, but because of that they expect a lot from their team. There's a tremendous tradition of football in the county, and his arrival was headline news.

I watched a lot of the trial matches he held at the start and in my opinion Kildare had a very, very ordinary bunch of players. He moulded them together, gave them confidence, and got them exceptionally fit. In the beginning, he got them winning matches against better teams because they were so fit. He got them to a league final, so fired up that they felt they could walk on water. After that he got them to two Leinster finals, but when they lost both, they ran him out of the county.

Unfortunately, Kildare had two bad years after that. His successor, Dermot Earley, was on a hiding to nothing. I think Dermot was expected to perform a miracle, but they got knocked out in the first round of the championship in consecutive years. The County Board realised the mistake they had made and brought O'Dwyer back. It was a difficult situation for him and he did an incredible job to lift that team. It was an amazing achievement, and I think he was unfortunate not to win an All-Ireland final in 1998 because of all the injuries they had in the run-up, though Galway gave a tremendous display on the day.

What is the recipe for success in football today?

You need a manager with very good organisational skills, who can identify and assemble a panel of twenty-five skilful players who are totally dedicated and committed. The manager has to have the full support and respect of the players in order to push them through the long hours of training.

'The game,' he thinks, 'is now gone semi-professional.'

Mangan has a vast reservoir of memories from his career, and of the great players he met on the pitch.

Mick O'Connell was a tremendous player. He played football as I believe it should be played; he concentrated on the ball and used his exceptional skills and fitness to outwit his opponent. One of the great skills of Gaelic football is catching the ball in the clouds, and O'Connell was an artist at this. He was also a superb kicker of the ball. He had a very sharp football brain, and in my opinion he was one of the all-time greats.

Brian Mullins would have been an ideal midfield partner for O'Connell — a great competitor and a tremendous worker. He wouldn't have the polished skills of O'Connell, but he was tremendously strong, a wonderful competitor who could catch with the best of them, and he had a tremendous will to win. They would have been unbeatable.

Another great player was Offaly's Willie Bryan, a class player who played football as it should be played. He never resorted to dirty play. Dermot Earley would be pretty similar to Willie Bryan, probably stronger than Willie and with a better work-rate. I also played against Galway's Jimmy Duggan, who was a lovely player and sheer class. He had a great pair of hands and was a great man to catch a ball.

Although he did not play on Sean O'Neill, Mangan is a huge admirer of the Down star.

Sean O'Neill was one of the greatest players I ever saw playing, and I had the pleasure of playing with him on the All-Star trip to San Francisco. He was a tremendous two-footed player with a great kick of the ball. A very intelligent competitor, his running off the ball was second to none, and his vision and accuracy was outstanding.

One other player who I have to mention is Mickey Kearins. We played Sligo a few times and he was fantastic. Maybe I'm being a bit unfair to the other players, but he carried the entire Sligo team for years. Although he is best known as a hurler, I played against Babs Keating a few times and he was a great footballer, not to mention a wonderful character.

Mangan's dream team, leaving out Kildare players, is as follows:

Billy Morgan (Cork)

Enda Colleran (Galway) John O'Keeffe (Kerry) Robbie Kelleher (Dublin)

Páidí Ó Sé (Kerry) Kevin Moran (Dublin) Martin Newell (Galway)

Mick O'Connell (Kerry) Brian Mullins (Dublin)

Mickey Kearins (Sligo) Matt Connor (Offaly) Pat Spillane (Kerry)

Colm O'Rourke (Meath) Sean O'Neill (Down) John Egan (Kerry)

Super Mac

Packy McGarty is the Jimmy Magee of Gaelic football. The centre-half forward on the team of greatest players never to have won an All-Ireland reels off entire teams from the last six decades with astonishing ease, and speaks about up-and-coming players from every county in Ireland with the familiarity of old friends.

Born in Mohill, Co. Leitrim, in 1933, his senior inter-county career began in 1949 and finished in 1971 when he was thirty-nine. He played in six senior Connacht finals without winning one of them, and reached the National League semi-final in the spring of 1959. The closest he came to glory was when Galway beat Leitrim by 2–10 to 1–11 in the 1958 Connacht final. McGarty was Leitrim's star, but the county had other good players too, like Cathal Flynn at corner-forward.

Football dominated Packy's life from an early age.

Football was all you had. Every evening as a boy I'd go with my friends to see the men training. We'd be hoping that the ball would go over the bar, and we'd be fighting just to get a kick of it.

Packy McGarty in relaxed mode.

As kids we did not have footballs, just a sock filled with grass. Listening to a match on a Sunday was the highlight of the week, because my father had fifteen shillings a week to keep a family of five of us.

We had a good teacher, Master Keegan from Offaly, who trained us in the skills of the game, with the result that we had a nice schoolboy team. We won the Leitrim championship at under-13 and under-14 level in 1946 and '47 respectively, and the Leitrim minor championship in 1950 and 1951. Apart from winning three Railway Cups, that was the end of my medals!

Leitrim had a good minor team in 1951 and Galway only beat us by a goal in the Connacht minor semi-final. They went on to beat Roscommon in the Connacht final, but Roscommon objected successfully because Galway had included an over-age player. We probably hadn't objected because we had an illegal player of our own! In 1952 Leitrim were regraded as a junior team and we lost the All-Ireland final in Tralee.

As a boy McGarty was a huge fan of the great Roscommon team of the 1940s.

Donal Keenan was one of the best men I ever saw to take a free. When I was fourteen I saw him play one of his last matches of his career in Carrick-on-Shannon. It was such a wet day, when there was a delay while Donal took a free from the sideline, they were throwing a coat on him to keep the rain off. Then he stepped up and slotted the ball between the posts. I said to myself, 'That's some free.'

Bill Carlos had legs like tree trunks. I also saw Brendan Lynch playing full-forward at the latter end of his career. He was like a tank. We never saw those great players, but Mícheál O'Hehir, who really made the GAA, turned them into superheroes. The first time I was brought to an All-Ireland was in 1948, and an hour before the train got to Dublin I was standing just to get my first glimpse of Croke Park. That was my dream come true.

Who was the biggest influence on his career?

It was Leo McAlinden from Armagh. He played at midfield for both his native county and Leitrim and for both Ulster and Connacht. He was a bank clerk and based in Mohill for a while. He was about six foot tall but very light looking, and the first time he came to play for the club nobody knew much about him, apart from one of the mentors, Jim McGann. The manager, as it were, Billy McGowan, said to Jim, 'That young buck, do you think we could stick him in at corner-forward? Do you think he'd get hurted? Some of those boys are as hard as nails.'

'He doesn't like to play corner-forward,' Jim replied.

'Well, he should be happy to get in there.'

Then Leo said in his strong Armagh accent, 'If it's all right with you, I'd like to start in the middle of the field, and if I'm not doing well I'll come off.'

Mother of God, once the game started they had never seen anything like him. He was soon the talk of the county. People were asking: 'Did you see that fella from Mohill? Where did he come from?' He had a massive impact on attendances in Leitrim because everyone wanted to see him play.

He could kick accurately with left or right. I imitated his solo-run. When he was going to meet his man, he would throw the ball one way and run the other. You don't see that skill so much now. He was a brilliant player. He had such skill and balance that he could throw a cigarette in the air and catch it with the tip of his toe.

I idolised him. One evening he asked me if I would carry his gear back to his digs because he wanted to meet his girlfriend. I had never felt so honoured: I was carrying Leo McAlinden's stuff!

I remember him playing in a derby club match when there was a very strong rivalry between the sides. Leo had his penalty saved by the goalie and he went in and shook his hand and congratulated him. You don't get men like that any more.

I played on him when he was at the end of his career and I was only a whipper-snapper, but I was quicker than him. Some fellas would get mad at you for that, but he didn't. After the match he shook my hand and said, 'Well done, young fella.' It gave me great confidence.

Tactics formed an important part of Packy's progression through the occasionally shark-infested waters of junior club football.

I started playing junior club football at corner-forward. We had a massive full-forward called Billy McGowan who was as strong as a

horse and would take half the defence down when he went for the ball.
As he knocked it down, I would race in and pop the ball over the bar,
and get the hell out of there as fast as I could. My father was chairman
of the club, and he always told me that if I stood around or held on to
the ball I would be killed. The opposition would go spare and start
screaming, 'Who's marking the garsún?' Someone said once, 'Well, if
he's a garsún he shouldn't be here.'

No one was more surprised than McGarty at his astonishingly
quick elevation to inter-county status.

I was selected for my first match for Leitrim when I was sixteen. I
didn't even know I was being picked. A fella came to the door the day
of my match and said: 'Where's your stuff?'
    'How do you mean?' I answered.
    'You're playing today.' I didn't believe him.

The game against Offaly 'went OK,' he recalls. 'I got a couple of
scores.'
He was only nineteen when he was selected to play for Connacht.

I'll always remember sitting in the back of the car on the way to the
match with Mayo's Padraic Carney, the 'Flying Doctor,' who was the
greatest footballer I ever saw. I was only a young lad from Leitrim and
I was going to be marking the Munster captain, Jas Murphy, who
captained Kerry to win the All-Ireland in 1953. He was six-foot-three
and I was only a small lad in comparison. I was thinking about this
when Padraic said, 'Junior, don't be afraid.' It gave me great confidence.
    Then just before we went out Padraic Carney put up his hands and
said, 'I have no authority to speak, lads, but I just want to say a couple
of words. It takes two points to beat one and there's no goalie over the
bar. A goal is the result of a mistake.'
    It made great sense. It's advice I often gave myself later. If you go
up the field early, get a point, spit on your hands, the confidence flows
through you as you face the kick-out. But it's an awful thing to go
down the field, go for a goal and miss it; then the opposition clear the
ball, score a point, and now it's you who are trailing.
    I remember getting a goal and four points on the day. A few days
before the match I got a splinter in my hand. I had a bandage on it and

was wearing gloves. The first ball that came into me I caught it and it fell out of my hand, and I caught it again and kicked it over the bar. I got rid of my gloves and bandage straight away, and as I was doing that Carney clapped me on the back and said, 'Well done, Junior.' I had one of my best games ever.

I also remember it was the first time I saw a blondy-haired young fella playing at right full-back for Connacht. It was Mayo's Willie Casey. He was a great player, and it was right that he was chosen on the centenary team of players who had never won an All-Ireland.

McGarty won his only national honours in Railway Cup football.

We won the Railway Cup in 1957 and '58 and were beaten by a point in the final in 1959. I missed it because I was working in England and got a 'flu because of the smog. I was disgusted, because I loved playing with Sean Purcell and Frank Stockwell.

That Galway team should have won the three-in-a-row after winning in 1956. They threw it away. Cork beat them by a point in the All-Ireland semi-final, mainly because the Galway midfield didn't play well on the day. Galway were over-confident. Then they lost the semi-final to Dublin in 1958 by a point, after twice nearly smashing the crossbar with what should have been goals.

McGarty won a third Railway Cup medal as a sub in 1967. Which was his most memorable match?

The game I recall most was a Connacht championship match against Sligo in 1956. I gave up everything to train for it; my work and holidays and everything. On the day, I was as stiff as a board and I couldn't move. I should have been taken off but I wasn't. If I'd played well we'd have won because all the other lads played well, but I was useless. Two months later I was playing in a factory league game and all the training paid off — I was running up and down the pitch like a gazelle.

What was his best game?

In 1957 we beat Leinster in the Railway Cup semi-final in Ballinasloe. I was on four different men on that day. I began by marking Gerry

O'Reilly of Wicklow, and when he was taken off Stephen White of
Louth was switched over on me, and later Jim McDonnell and Paddy
Gibbons of Kildare. Cathal Flynn and I got the entire Connacht tally,
apart from two points scored by Sean Purcell. I couldn't do anything
wrong on the day.

At the time, I would never wear boots in a match unless I had
worn them for about three months in training, but as we were getting
ready to travel to the match, I left my gear behind me and it was
stolen. A fella from Ballinasloe, Jack Wood, had an old pair of boots
that fitted me and seemed OK. My Sean McDermott's clubmate, Kevin
Beahan, gave me a pair of old socks and Gerry O'Malley had an extra
pair of togs which he loaned to me. I went out with strange boots, togs
and socks and played the game of my life!

McGarty always thought deeply about the game, and there
were many occasions when Leitrim reaped the reward for this.

George Geraghty of Roscommon was an All-Ireland Colleges
champion high-jumper. I vividly remember the first time I ever saw
him play. He was selected for my club, Sean McDermott's, at midfield.
Although I wasn't a big man I loved jumping for the ball and could
reach a fair height. I went up for the ball once that day and had my
hand on it when somebody soared in like a bird and took it off me. It
was my own team-mate, George. We were playing Roscommon the
following Sunday in the Connacht championship, and I knew we
would be in big trouble, because they had both George and Gerry
O'Malley at midfield.

That whole week I spent thinking about how we would stop
George; I knew we wouldn't be able to stop O'Malley no matter what
plan we came up with. At half-time we were leading Roscommon by
eight points to three, but twenty minutes into the second half it was
8–8 and George and O'Malley were lording it at midfield. I decided to
go to centrefield. I had a plan in my mind. As the ball was cleared out,
George was winning everything by running up and catching it, so I
would back into him and stop him running, and when the ball was
about to drop I'd sprint out and catch it. We won by eleven points to
nine. The next morning the headline in the paper was, 'Super Switch
by Leitrim Wins Game.' The thing was, Leitrim didn't know a thing

about it! I told George later that the biggest mistake he ever made was playing for Sean McDermott's the week before, because I knew his form then.

Probably the most revealing insight into McGarty's make-up comes when he is asked about the biggest regret of his career. It is not his failure to win an All-Ireland, nor even a Connacht medal.

In one of my first matches for Leitrim, I was marking Brian O'Reilly of Cavan and I gave him an elbow in the ribs. He just looked at me and said, 'I play football.' I've never felt so ashamed of myself. It was a lesson I never forgot about how to play the game.

Cavan's sole representative on the 1984 centenary team of greatest players never to have won an All-Ireland medal at right corner-forward, Charlie Gallagher, tops McGarty's list of great characters in the game.

I went to America for the Kennedy games in 1964 with the late Charlie, and Gerry O'Malley. They were like chalk and cheese: O'Malley was very serious, religious and quiet; Charlie was devil-may-care, yet they became amazingly close on the trip. They were a panto-mime. Gerry O'Malley had to win every match he played, and Gallagher was always winding him up, saying that if they ever met in a match he would destroy him. This drove O'Malley mad, though in private Charlie admitted that he would have hated to have to play on him.

At first he asks to be excused from selecting his dream team.

When I was young and going to Croke Park there were always great arguments about who had the best half-back line of all time: the Roscommon half-back line of 1943–44 with Brendan Lynch, Bill Carlos and Phelim Murray, or the Cavan back line of 1947–48. I can still hear Mícheál O'Hehir calling them out: 'On the right is P.J. Duke, in the centre Commandant John Joe O'Reilly, and on the left Lieutenant Simon Deignan.' And there have been so many great half-backs since, how could you possibly pick the best half-back line never mind the greatest team of all time? There were so many great forwards too, like Tom Langan, Sean O'Neill, Sean Purcell and Kevin Heffernan.

Nonetheless, eventually he was persuaded to select a side from his own era.

Johnny Geraghty (Galway)
Jerome O'Shea (Kerry) Paddy Prendergast (Mayo) Tom O'Hare (Down)
Sean Murphy (Kerry) Gerry O'Malley (Roscommon) Stephen White (Louth)
Padraic Carney (Mayo) Jim McKeever (Derry)
Sean O'Neill (Down) Sean Purcell (Galway) Paddy Doherty (Down)
Denis Kelleher (Cork) Tom Langan (Mayo) Kevin Heffernan (Dublin)

On Guard

The history of the GAA is studded with personalities who have retained forever a niche in the memory of those who have had the good fortune to see them in action. Burrishoole and Mayo's goal-scoring supremo Willie McGee is such a player.

Detective Superintendent McGee of the Garda Fraud Squad cuts an imposing figure. Born in Newport in Mayo, an area identified as a handball stronghold, his childhood hero was 'the Flying Doctor,' Padraic Carney. He played minor for two years with the county before exploding on the national scene as a nineteen-year-old. In the All-Ireland under-21 football final replay of 1967 he really made his name for Mayo in their win over Kerry, scoring four golden goals.

Willie McGee bows his head before the adulation of Paddy Bluett (RIP), one of the great followers of Mayo football.

After scoring the goals I was put straight into the senior team. We won the Grounds tournament immediately, and my first league game was against Clare. I worked for four hours in the morning from six to ten and then drove to Kilrush, a journey of 180 miles. I togged out for Mayo and was playing on a big, hard full-back named Kennedy, and the game was only five minutes old when he hit me so hard I dislocated my shoulder. I was out of action all that winter.

He played a lot of handball to strengthen his shoulder, and eighteen months later his fortunes took a turn for the better when Mayo won the Connacht championship for the first and only time in his career. They went on to lose the All-Ireland semi-final to Kerry by just one point, a defeat that still rankles with McGee. He recalls:

A day or two later, Joe Sherwood wrote in the Evening Press *that my marker, Seamus Fitzgerald, who subsequently became a Kerry selector, would have been sent off three times if we were playing basketball, he fouled me so often. With a minute to go and us tailing by a point, John Morley sent in a long ball. I got possession and showed Fitzgerald a clear pair of heels, but he tapped me on the back of the ankle and brought me down. Seamus O'Dowd took the free, which was about fourteen yards out and to the right of the post, but unfortunately he sent it wide.*

It wasn't my biggest disappointment. That had come in 1965 when we were a very fancied minor team and Roscommon beat us by 2–10 to 1–10 in the Connacht championship in Tuam. At that time they had started televising the All-Ireland semi-finals, including the minor match, and we were all looking forward to being on live television. We had won the Connacht league that year quite easily and when we played Roscommon in the championship we were expected to beat them easily. Dermot Earley was playing great football at the time and practically beat us on his own. That defeat had the biggest impact on me, and I think that because I experienced defeat so young, it made me more philosophical.

That same year I was brought on to the Connacht team in the Railway Cup semi-final as a substitute in the last fifteen minutes. Connacht were losing at the time. I got the winning goal in the last few minutes, which meant I got my place in the side for the final, and we won. The next day I was on duty in Pearse Street and I got one of the first editions of the Irish Press *that morning. It was a great thrill to see a picture of the winning Connacht side and then to read that we were getting a trip to New York to play in the Cardinal Cushing games as a result.*

In 1970 he scored a goal in the first five minutes of the first half and another in the first five minutes of the second to help Mayo beat Offaly in the league semi-final. His opponent was the legendary Paddy McCormack. Then came the high point of his inter-county career: the National League final against Down.

I had three stitches in my eye — I accidentally bumped into a fella in a soccer game — and I can't recall that much of it. We were all so excited about winning, maybe that blurred the memory. The one thing I can recall from the match is John Gibbons sending in a high ball. I was standing in front of the goalkeeper and I went to catch it, sold a dummy in the air, and the ball went straight into the net. The thing was, I never got any credit for it. I can't repeat to you what the goalie said to me!

That was the first of three consecutive league finals for Mayo, though they lost the next two to Kerry.

We thought that was the start of a great new chapter in Mayo's history. We went to play Galway in the first round of the championship and we were absolutely flying, but Galway caught us on the hop. It was a lesson, even though we had been reminded of it beforehand, that League doesn't equate with Championship. After defeating Down we weren't ready for Galway because it was the first success in Mayo for years and we got carried away. Mayo always had a big problem coping with being favourites and never lost it! I think, too, that Mayo's style of football is that they go out to please rather than to win. They never had that 'win at all cost' mentality bred into them.

McGee was the most prolific goal-scorer in Gaelic football, apart from Mikey Sheehy, and the Kerry ace had the not inconsiderable advantage of being the penalty-taker on a great team to boost his tally. What made him the Jimmy Greaves of football?

I had a knack of being able to fall down when I was kicking the ball, and when you do that it's very hard to block down your kick. I was also told that I used throw the ball down on my foot faster than normal.

In 1976 injury saw the end of Willie McGee's career when he was still in his twenties. Just the year before, when they lost to Sligo in the Connacht final replay, he had been Mayo captain.

Our manager had decided on a live-in weekend in St Muirdeach's College in Ballina. After a training session and a match on the Saturday, we were all in good form and we had a basketball match. I went up for a high ball and as I came down I got a nudge and twisted my ankle, tore a ligament, tore away a piece of the bone in my ankle, and that finished my inter-county career.

I got back to fitness after three operations on my ankle. I made myself available to the county after playing a representative game for the Gardaí against the Universities, when I scored 1–4 on the then Kildare full-back, Paddy O'Donoghue. I had everything to lose by going back. People like Mick O'Dwyer, Mick O'Connell and Paddy McCormack had done so without great success. You were on a hiding to nothing if you came out of retirement and your side still lost. I was fitter than when I had been playing; I had finally realised the importance of training hard, and I was training like I never trained before. But I was married and had a mortgage and I was a Garda who often had to work on Sundays, so it was just a question of being paid a proper allowance. Unfortunately, we couldn't come to an agreement on that.

It was not the first time McGee had had a disagreement with the football authorities in Mayo.

I remember getting into trouble with the County Board about playing in New York without getting permission, and they suspended me. I told the County Board chairman I was just ignorant of the rules. He told me to put it in writing, but I answered back that they hadn't put it in writing when they suspended me, and if word of mouth was good enough for them it ought to be good enough for me! There was a stand-off position for a while, and then one day I was on duty in Grafton Street when a priest, Fr Paddy Mahon, met me. He followed me up and down the beat for an hour in order to persuade me to change my mind. Eventually I relented. I wrote my piece [to the County Board] on the back of a cigarette box.

A short while later I had occasion to go to England for work reasons. I was seen in the airport heading for departures at the same time as a plane to America was called, and I was reported to the County Board. I was duly asked if I was playing in New York. Given my previous experience, I told them to come back to me when they had evidence. I didn't make them any the wiser whether I had played or not.

McGee had reason to be worried about being reported on another occasion.

When I first started playing championship football the ban was still in operation, so you daren't be seen at a soccer or rugby match, or play them either. I vividly remember attending a soccer match in Dalymount Park one day when I heard this chant, 'Burrishoole, Burrishoole!' coming from behind the goal. I lifted my collar up to hide my face because I was scared stiff of being reported, but it was a Roscommon man, Noel Carthy, who is a good friend of mine. I was glad to know it was him.

Since his retirement, McGee has noted a number of significant changes in the game. 'There are plus sides,' he says. 'I think the fast free kick from the hand speeds up the game and makes for better entertainment value.' But not all the changes are for the better.

Teams of my era didn't train half as much as they do today, though we probably did more ball work. I think back to the 1997 All-Ireland final between Kerry and Mayo, and I was very disappointed by the level of ball control from both sides. The name of the game is football and that's why we go to see matches, not to watch guys running. I think in my time there was a better standard of footballing skills.

He is also disappointed by the level of aggression that sometimes mars the game.

Because teams train more they're probably more likely to wade in and defend their colleague, which sometimes leads to a free-for-all.

There is also a lot of pressure on managers to win, which is fuelled by the media. We have a situation that for a successful manager there can be handsome rewards. Let's be honest about it, a successful manager can make a lot of money nowadays, so that adds to the pressure.

When Mayo football lost its focus after a highly publicised squabble between the management and the players in 1992, McGee was recruited in a campaign to take corrective action.

I felt at the time that Jack O'Shea was the man to bring some good days back to the county. Some people close to the top in Mayo football had the same view and I was asked by the chairman of the County Board, Christy Loftus, to raise the funds from the friends of Mayo in Dublin and to personally approach Jacko to take on the Mayo job. To be fair to him, I think that given the travel involved he deserved to be properly looked after. Things didn't work out the way people hoped, however, and again we raised the funds to be able to offer the post to John Maughan.

McGee was himself involved for a time in training some of Mayo's Dublin-based county players, such as Liam MacHale and Anthony 'Fat Larry' Finnerty, one of the great characters of Mayo football. During Brian McDonald's tenure as trainer some years later, the former Dublin player was taking a training session and had the players jogging around the pitch. He told them that every time he blew his whistle they were to jump high in the air and imagine they were catching a high ball. This drill went on around the field, but when they got level with the dressing-rooms Finnerty made a beeline towards them. 'Where are you going?' the trainer shouted.

'I'm just going in to get my gloves,' Fat Larry replied. 'That bloody ball you want us to catch is very slippery!'

McGee's talents as a player were publicly acknowledged when he was nominated as one of the ten full-forwards for a place on the Team of the Century in 1984. The position in fact went to another Mayo man, Tom Langan, but the nomination was nonetheless 'a great honour'. McGee was subsequently picked on the centenary team of greatest players who never won an All-Ireland. When he heard the news he thought it was a prank, and admits, 'I didn't expect to be selected.'

McGee himself is a great admirer of many former greats, none more so than Mick O'Connell,

especially as Kerry beat us in the All-Ireland semi-final and two league finals and he played so well against us on all three occasions. He was always very fit and loved playing against Mayo because we never set out to hurt him or take him out of the game. Mayo tried to play football with him and as a result we always came out second best. He was the best footballer I ever saw.

He was a great fielder of a ball, as was Noel Tierney and P.J. Loftus, and I think that I never saw anybody give as good an exhibition of fielding as Willie Joe Padden gave for Mayo against Dublin in the replay of the 1985 All-Ireland semi-final. The difference was that none of them could touch Mick O'Connell for distributing the ball.

McGee's dream team was:

Johnny Geraghty (Galway)
Johnny Carey (Mayo) Noel Tierney (Galway) Paddy McCormack (Offaly)
John Donnellan (Galway) John Morley (Mayo) Gerry O'Malley (Roscommon)
Mick O'Connell (Kerry) Dermot Earley (Roscommon)
Packy McGarty (Leitrim) Pat Griffin (Kerry) Micheál Kearins (Sligo)
John Egan (Kerry) Sean O'Neill (Down) Jimmy Keaveney (Dublin)

PRINCE AMONG THOROUGHBREDS

Peter McGinnity's portrait hangs among the 'unsung heroes' in Croke Park's magnificent new Gaelic games museum. McGinnity played his last senior game for Fermanagh in 1988, ending a nineteen-year career with the county which began when he was seventeen. He played on two successive under-21 teams beaten in the All-Ireland final, in 1970, when he was only sixteen, and 1971. With his brother, Gerry, partnering him in midfield, in 1977 he helped Fermanagh to capture the Dr McKenna Cup for the first time in forty-four years. He won four Railway Cup medals and became the only Fermanagh player ever to win an All-Star when he was selected at right half-forward in 1982.

Although he was starved of success with Fermanagh, he had a very different experience with his club.

My club was Roslea Shamrocks. Growing up in Roslea, the parish and the GAA club were almost interchangeable, though I played absolutely no football until I went to St Michael's College and never even togged out. I went to study in Belfast in 1972 and transferred to St John's there. We won three Antrim Senior Football Championship and League medals. I won an Ulster club medal and we lost the All-Ireland final to Thomond College. I moved back to teach in St Michael's in 1979 and transferred back to Roslea. From 1980 to 1986 we won six leagues, three championships and reached an Ulster club final. There were a few disappointments on the way, especially the county finals in 1987 and 1989. The last one was a big downer for me because I missed a penalty with the last kick of the game, when we were only one point down.

What made the missed penalty even more disappointing was that place-kicking had always been one of McGinnity's great talents.

One of the most formative influences in my career, James Lynch, once invited the legendary Cavan player Mick Higgins to come along to an under-16 training session in Roslea. He saw that I was the free-taker, so he came up and showed me how to set the ball with the laces facing the goals, the idea being that the weight at that point would draw it towards the goals. From that day on I always did as he advised, and when the laces went I even set the ball with the little nipple facing the goals.

McGinnity met Higgins again on one of the proudest days of his career, his debut for Ulster against the Combined Universities in 1973. Higgins was manager of the Ulster side.

I remember my first match especially because there were two other Fermanagh players on the team with me, Kieran Campbell and Phil Sheridan, which was our highest representation ever, as well as having Finn Sherry play for the Combined Universities. Four Fermanagh lads playing inter-provincial football on the one day was big news!

When we went into the dressing-room first, the manager said to me, 'Here you are, Kieran, here's the number 3 jersey,' and then he turned to Kieran Campbell and said, 'Here's your number 10 jersey.' It pulled us down a peg or two not be recognised by Mick Higgins!

The six-foot-three midfielder produced many outstanding performances throughout his career, and regards the 1982 Ulster semifinal between Fermanagh and Tyrone as the highlight.

We went into that game as underdogs, having beaten

Peter McGinnity with the New York Gold Cup after leading Roslea to the Fermanagh senior football final.

Derry by a single point in the first round. Just before the match our captain, Arthur McCaffrey, cried off with 'flu, so as vice-captain I took over for the day. I still remember leading the Fermanagh team around in pouring rain.

Despite the weather, the game turned into

one of those dream days when you think nothing can go wrong for you. I especially recall scoring a point from forty yards out and into the wind, when I had no right even to be trying to score. I couldn't believe it when the ball sailed over the bar. Ultimately, though, what mattered most was that it was a great day for Fermanagh.

Unlike a great Fermanagh forward of the 1960s, P.T. Treacy, also a candidate for the soubriquet 'the greatest player never to win an All-Ireland medal,' McGinnity at least got the opportunity to play in an Ulster final, though they lost to Armagh by two points. 'They say time heals all wounds, but the passing years haven't washed away that bitter disappointment,' he says.

The biggest influence on Peter's career was Mick Brewster, his teacher and coach at St Michael's, Enniskillen. Now the wheel has come the full circle and Peter teaches and trains in St Michael's. After his retirement from the playing fields, McGinnity was snapped up by the BBC to cover the Ulster championships with former Armagh star Jimmy Smyth.

When my playing days with Fermanagh were coming to an end, I became player–manager. It was a stop-gap measure. I had been captaining the team and I thought it would be a natural progression for me to become a player–manager, but I was very wrong. I don't think the player–manager system can work. I was too close to the players and I wasn't prepared for the politics that goes on behind the scenes in terms of clubs wanting their players on the team. I was glad to be finished with it, and I made it clear then that I didn't want to go through the experience again.

Yet he was persuaded to take the job of managing Leitrim. 'Persuaded is the key word,' he explains.

The Leitrim county secretary, Tommy Moran, more or less made it clear to me that he was going to keep hounding me until I accepted the job.

It was a real learning experience, seeing the changes that have taken place in the game even in the ten years since I had stopped playing. It's become a lot more scientific now and much more time-consuming for both the players and the manager. I also learned that you need great man-management skills to have a successful team. In recent years, the two men that stand out in this respect would be Down's Pete McGrath and Meath's Sean Boylan, in terms of the success they have had in getting the best out of players who would be perceived from the outside as being difficult. I always was told that if you had organisation and money you were on the road to success, but I was to learn that you need the players as well.

He stepped down abruptly from his Leitrim post. 'In the early months of 1999 I was having serious health problems,' he says.

I was coaching a group of young fellas one day and a ball struck me on the side of my head. It left me with a detached retina, which required major surgery. It got detached again in July 1999. So the fact that my general health was not good was one of the factors.

Leitrim were in a very difficult section in the league and we were having major problems with illness and injury. I felt if we got just one win we would turn the corner. Before Christmas we drew with Tyrone in a game we should have won, and I thought that might do it, but after Christmas we slumped again.

A county with a playing base as small as Leitrim's will only get success in cycles. They'll always have good players but it's not often they will have enough of them to make a good team. Leitrim were in that situation from 1990 to 1994, but with all the miles they had to clock up going to train, the end had really come for the 1994 team. Declan Darcy's switch to Dublin was a huge loss. I felt in those circumstances that we had to start from scratch and do new things, but there were those living on the memory of 1994 who felt we should continue on with the old ways.

After Christmas 1999 I no longer seemed to be able to get the players to do what I wanted. What was happening on the pitch bore no relation to what I had planned. Things came to a head when we played Offaly in the league. By their own admission they played very poorly on the day: the game was there for the taking, but we didn't take it. After that, my two selectors and I decided we couldn't take the team any further.

Who was the greatest player he ever saw?

I've often been asked that question and I've always answered by saying that there were many great players but the one I respected most was Offaly's Matt Connor. When the chips were down, he rose to the occasion. Some players, like myself, could do it when the team is winning by twenty points, but I saw him in a Railway Cup final in Breffni Park in 1983 when Ulster seemed to have won it and Leinster needed a goal. He manufactured a goal from his own twenty-five-yard line and finished by scoring it at the other end. His free-taking ability and point-taking from play with either foot was something else.

Apart from Matt, another player I'd have to mention is Kerry's Maurice Fitzgerald. I saw him play for Kerry against Fermanagh in Enniskillen and he was the complete player. He scored 1–5, including points from play with both feet, caught some magnificent balls in the centre of the field and defended well.

Another Kerry player springs to mind when he thinks of his most difficult opponents.

Playing on Jack O'Shea was great. Brian Mullins was a great player to play against, because he would play his own game, but then, if the notion took him, he could stop you playing. I would have to say, though, that the player I found toughest of all was in club football, Paddy Reilly from Teemore Shamrocks. In the late '70s and early '80s, no matter what game I played against him I had serious problems.

One of the funniest incidents in my career happened when I was marking Paddy. Paddy's brother, Barney, enjoys the rare distinction of having won senior county medals in four different decades: in the 1960s, 1970s and 1980s with Teemore, and a Meath medal in the early 1990s with Navan O'Mahony's. Barney and I played for Fermanagh under-21s and came up the ranks together, and I always had great time for him.

In one club match, the ball went up between Paddy and myself and a kind of ruck developed. I snatched the ball as Barney came charging in to give Paddy some 'assistance', and happily for me, but not for Paddy, in the confusion Barney struck his own brother instead of me. As I was heading up the field with the ball I heard Barney say, 'Sorry, Paddy,' as his brother lay stretched out on the ground, and then he started up the field after me.

He prefaces his dream team selection by referring to the difficulty of picking players from different eras, and decides to include one player he never saw playing, having heard much about his exploits as a player: Sean Purcell.

One other player in this category who very nearly made my team was Derry's Jim McKeever. He was my coach at college, and my earliest football memory is listening to big games on the radio back in 1958, and it almost always seemed to be that Jim McKeever was on the ball. So when I started playing imaginary games as a very young boy, I was always, 'Jim McKeever on the ball.'

Brian McAlinden (Armagh)
Robbie O'Malley (Meath) John O'Keeffe (Kerry) Páidí Ó Sé (Kerry)
Paddy Moriarty (Armagh) Kevin Moran (Dublin) Henry Downey (Derry)
Jack O'Shea (Kerry) Brian Mullins (Dublin)
Sean O'Neill (Down) Sean Purcell (Galway) Matt Connor (Offaly)
Jimmy Barry-Murphy (Cork) Eoin Liston (Kerry) Nudie Hughes (Monaghan)

Jim'll Fix It

In 1958 the GAA world witnessed a shock of seismic proportions when Derry beat Kerry by 2–6 to 2–5 in the All-Ireland semi-final. The Foylesiders were led to the promised land by a prince among midfielders, Jim McKeever. McKeever's ability to jump and catch the ball were the hallmarks of his play. Extended from toes to fingertips as he grabbed the ball, he would hit the ground, turn and play. One of his most famous feats of fielding was caught on camera and is replayed in all good coaching manuals under the title, 'The Catch'. McKeever's mastery of his position was recognised in 1984 when he was chosen at centrefield on the centenary team of greatest players never to have won an All-Ireland, partnering the legendary Tommy 'The Boy Wonder' Murphy of Laois.

Born in Ballymaguigan in 1930, McKeever's love of football was nurtured by his father, who brought him on the bar of his bike to games. He was still a boy when he made his senior debut for Derry at the age of seventeen.

> I remember listening to the famous All-Ireland final in the Polo Grounds, New York, in 1947. I didn't think then that a year later I'd be playing in a challenge game for the county against Antrim. It wasn't until the following year that I made my championship debut. When I was in my teens, Derry used to play in the junior championship; we didn't have a senior team then. At that stage there was a tremendous gap between Cavan and Antrim and the other seven counties in Ulster. We played in the Lagan Cup, which featured the eight counties in Ulster apart from Cavan.

A major impediment to Derry's advancement was the fact that its footballing base was so narrow. It also lacked the foundation of a strong colleges' scene.

I believe that success in football or hurling is largely determined by population. When the playing population is small, you are always struggling to fill in the last three or four places. And you need to be a big school to have a successful colleges side. St Columb's in Derry had a great team in the 1960s, but as a boarding school they were mainly powered by players outside the city. Derry was a soccer stronghold too, which was a big disadvantage for us. By the law of averages, given the population of the city it should be providing about forty to fifty per cent of the team, but it has given us nowhere near that. The ban worked very badly against us in Derry.

Sport, religion, race and politics were inextricably twined together in Derry. Poet Seamus Heaney writes of the way walking through the streets on Ash Wednesday, a badge of ashes on one's forehead, heightened one's sense of caste. Similarly, the green chestnut tree that flourished at the entrance to the GAA grounds was more abundantly green for being the peak from which the tricolour was flown illegally at Easter. For the city's GAA faithful, football was central to their identity, an essential element in the fabric of their lives.

McKeever's first brush with glory came in 1950.

We played in an All-Ireland Junior Football Championship final, only to be beaten by Mayo. I played against a young Mick Loftus. I think it was my first time playing in Croke Park. Croke Park was the cathedral, and travelling to Dublin and

Jim McKeever on the ball.

staying overnight was a big thrill, almost as wonderful an occasion as
playing in a senior final.

McKeever's reputation soon soared and representative honours
followed quickly.

The Railway Cup was a big thing at the time. It attracted massive
attendances; there were crowds of 25–30,000 in every game I played.
The emphasis was on playing the best football. It was great for
footballers in the weaker counties to play against the very best, and
everybody wanted to win. I think it's a great pity that the competition
went into such decline. The first Railway Cup match I played in, I was
marking the great Mayo captain, Sean Flanagan. In the second year I
marked the legendary Paddy Bawn Brosnan of Kerry. The reputation
of players like that tended to emphasise their toughness or hardness, but
I found nothing untoward happened.

Paddy Bawn was one of the game's tough characters, but there
were moments in his career when the macho mask occasionally
slipped. One wet Sunday, Kerry were playing Clare in a league
fixture on a waterlogged pitch when 'the Bawn' was blinded by a
splash of water. When he called for a towel, Kerry trainer Jackie
Lyne took if from the baggage man and stuck it in the mud before
passing it on, and when the Bawn rubbed his face of course he
ended up making it ten times worse. The players collapsed with
laughter, though nobody enjoyed the pantomime more than Paddy.
The high point of McKeever's career came against Kerry in 1958.

I have no recollection of great excitement when we won the Ulster
final. However, when we beat Kerry in the All-Ireland semi-final the
response was sensational. I remember the great John Joe Sheehy saying
to me, 'That's a rattling good team you have there.'

However, despite a magnificent display from McKeever in
midfield, Dublin beat Derry by 2–12 to 1–9 in the All-Ireland final.

I have no recollection of any great disappointment when we lost the
final to Dublin. We were happy just to be there. If someone had told us
a few years before that we would play in an All-Ireland final, we
would have been absolutely delighted.

Much to the chagrin of some Dublin supporters, who felt that the honour should have gone to one of their stars, McKeever was chosen as footballer of the year, an unprecedented honour for a player whose county had not won the All-Ireland title. 'I felt very honoured to win the award,' he recollects, 'not just for myself, but for my county, and I wasn't aware of any begrudgery towards me at the time.'

In 1960 and 1961 McKeever led Derry to the National League final, which they lost both times to Kerry. Finally, in 1963 he decided to call it a day. Ranging now over the highs and lows of football, it is not his own achievements which ignite the passion in his voice but his vivid description of the juvenile club match he had watched the evening before in Derry. Derry's first All-Ireland win in 1993 was a source of great pride to him.

It was very emotional when the full-time whistle went. The magnificent players on that team personified not only their own accomplishments but the sacrifices of generations of Derry people who made that moment possible. I was very conscious of all the people who organised games and travelling arrangements down through the years; without them, the sequence which led to Derry's historic success would not have started. All the years of disappointment were wiped out with the 1993 side's victory. It was a unique occasion. The first time that something great happens is special, because there can never be another first time.

Who was the greatest player of them all?

It's so difficult to judge. The greatest fielder and the most stylish footballer was definitely Mick O'Connell.

Who was his most difficult opponent?

One of the toughest guys to play against was Galway's Frank Eivers. He was just massive. You couldn't get near the ball with him standing there beside you.

After his playing days were over, McKeever went on to become a trainer and manager with both St Joseph's College and Derry.

I didn't enjoy it near as much as playing. Of course, it's a great buzz when you win, but it can be very, very demoralising when you lose and you know your team has passed its peak. I know there are a lot of people interested in administration, but it was never for me. I don't think people appreciate how much stress is on the manager, especially trying to do the job in your free time. Anybody who says it's easy is not talking about the job I recognise.

McKeever thinks deeply about the game and his discourse ranges from the need for ethics in sport to the importance of the Sigerson Cup and the precision of the late Mayo star John Morley's left foot. He remarks on some of the major changes in the game since his own playing days.

'I think the players of today are better than the players of my time in terms of fitness but not in terms of the skills. It takes a team five years to develop,' he thinks, and decries the fact that 'Nowadays, a bit of a 'win at all cost' mentality has crept in to the game. Only experienced players can handle that.'

He has many happy memories from his playing days, though he looks back also with a tinge of regret.

I enjoyed every moment of my playing career. The 1950s was the wrong time to be playing football because each year there were seven or eight counties who could have won the All-Ireland, which naturally made it difficult for counties like Derry to make the breakthrough. If I had to do it all again, I would take it a lot more seriously. I think we could have won an All-Ireland if we had really given it everything.

Many of his happiest memories are of the club scene:

Ballymaguigan were playing Coleraine in a club game in Coleraine and the pitch wasn't very well marked, the crossbar was only a rope and there weren't any nets. Once when the ball was bobbing around in the square, somebody pulled on the rope, and one umpire gave a goal, the other a point. The referee split the difference and awarded two points. The really comic part of the story was that one of our best players, the late Michael Young, did not want to play as he had hay ready for baling and the weather forecast was not good. He was persuaded to play, but when the controversy broke out Young went up to the referee and told him that he should hurry up and make a decision, as he had to go home to bale the hay!

McKnight Moves

John McKnight began playing football in street and altar boy leagues in his home town, Newry, Co. Armagh, and at school in the local CBS. 'My father had a business in Newry,' John recalls,

> *but he took a field outside the town and kept a few cows in it for the milk; my mother churned it into butter. There was a flat corner in the field and we played a lot of football there.*
>
> *The Cavan team was the one to be feared at the time, although Armagh were the only county then who would always give them a good match. When we were in secondary school, all of us were packed into the library to hear the commentary of the All-Ireland final from the Polo Grounds in 1947. The game made a big impression on me as a youngster. All my heroes were Cavan players.*

As a player with Armagh, McKnight himself had few peers, a fact reflected in his selection at left full-back on the centenary team of the greatest players never to have won an All-Ireland medal.

> *I played minor for two years with Armagh and we won the All-Ireland in 1949. I was at school in St Pat's, Armagh, and in the previous two years Tyrone, powered by Eddie Delvin, had won the minor All-Ireland. There were a lot of Tyrone boys in our school and this gave us a great determination to take their crown off them. It was a momentous occasion. The turning point of the game was when our captain, Sean Blaney (later the father of Down star, Greg Blaney) got the ball a long way out, soloed through and put the ball into the net. As the years go by, that solo run gets longer and longer!*

McKnight made the breakthrough with the Armagh junior team in 1951 and won an Ulster junior championship medal in the same year. Opportunities to play for the senior team quickly followed.

I started getting games with the senior team after that, and I was a permanent fixture by 1953. My first year with the team, we got to the All-Ireland final!

Armagh beat Roscommon in the semi-final and faced Kerry in Croke Park.

The county went wild. We were the first team from the six counties to get to the final and that, by our standards, was a great achievement. I think that was probably the wrong attitude, in a sense, because we thought, 'It's great to be here, and if we win it, even better.' We should have gone in there thinking, 'This is our title and let's go out and claim it.' Even so, defeat [by four points] was hard to take, especially because we missed a penalty.

The ball had been kicked in by Brian Sealey and our fellas maintained that the Kerry goalie, Johnny Foley, carried the ball over the line. The umpires didn't flag it but Peter 'The Man in the Cap' McDermott gave a penalty. McDermott also refereed the final three years later, having captained Meath to win the All-Ireland in 1954, and in the process became the only man in history to have refereed an All-Ireland final before and after winning one as a player.

'Billy McCorry took the penalty,' McKnight continues.

He was a great man to take a penalty and had never missed one before. I think Billy's attitude was that he was going to put the goalkeeper, ball and all behind the line.

Some said McCorry missed the spot kick because a Kerry player upset his run-up to the ball. Ironically, Armagh were at the opposite end of such a controversy in the 1977 All-Ireland semi-final against Roscommon, when with the score tied at 3–9 to 2–12, Dermot Earley lined up a placed ball, the last kick of the game. Just as he faced the ball, Armagh trainer Gerry Neill ran across the field in front of him and shouted something, and the kick sailed high and wide. There was much press comment on the 'O'Neill-Earley' incident in the following days.

Armagh won the replay by a point, but history repeated itself in the final against Dublin in 1977, when Paddy Moriarty had a penalty saved by Dublin goalkeeper Paddy Cullen. Moriarty was reminded of the link between the two penalties, when, at Bill McCorry's funeral, someone remarked to him, 'How does it feel to be the only Armagh man alive to have missed a penalty in an All-Ireland final?'

Though they failed to win All-Ireland glory in 1953, the clash between Roscommon and Armagh in the semi-final that year provided McKnight with what he still considers to be his finest game.

It was one of those days when everything went well for me. The match was on the ninth of August and the following day was my twenty-first birthday. We won by a point. I started off marking Michael Regan (who was drowned shortly after that). In the second half he was moved out to the half-forward line and John Joe Nerney came into the corner. My clearest memory of the game was of Jack McQuillan coming on as a sub late in the game because he was marking me and he gave me a clatter!

Which game does he remember least fondly in terms of his own performance? 'I had a few of them!' he says.

I remember once marking Mayo's Joe Langan. For the first twenty minutes everything was going perfect for me. Then he started doing flicks and punching the ball away from me and set up goals and points all over the place. He really ruined that day for me!

Who was his most difficult opponent?

One fella I found very difficult was Seamus Hetherton, a priest from Tyrone. In the later years of my career, Cavan's Charlie Gallagher always gave me problems. At intervarsity level, one man who was very hard to play on was Peadar Kearins from UCG.

Why did Armagh not build on the success of 1953?

We lost the Ulster final in 1954 to Cavan. We thought we had a better team in 1954 because we had an experienced team. As it turned out, Meath beat Cavan in the All-Ireland semi-final and walloped Kerry in the final, so maybe if we had beaten Cavan we could have gone all the

*way. We had much the same team as the previous year, but it's so
difficult to come out of Ulster two years in a row.*

*You also have to bear in mind that the GAA population in
Armagh is quite restricted. There is not much support for Armagh
football in certain parts of Portadown!*

Although only one Ulster medal was to come his way, there
were other honours.

*I played with UCD with the likes of Eddie Delvin, Jim McDonnell and
James Brady of Cavan, and we won the Sigerson a couple of times. I
played for the Combined Universities when we beat the Rest of Ireland.
Those were great matches because the standard was very high, but the
competition started to sink when the Railway Cup grew in strength. I
won one Railway Cup. I played with Ulster for about five years, but I
made the mistake of playing one year when I was not fit because I was
doing my finals, and I was never asked to play for Ulster again.*

McKnight has no difficulty putting such disappointments into
perspective. He recalls a fellow Ulster footballer, Jim Delvin, who

*went to school in St Patrick's, Armagh, like me. The last time I played
for Ulster, Jim was full-back. He was shot with his wife in Coalisland
by Loyalists during the height of the Troubles.*

McKnight is deeply involved in the GAA, both in his work and
through marriage. He has been the GAA's solicitor for thirty
years, and his family is closely connected to the great Down team
of the early 1960s.

*My sister, Mary, is married to Kevin O'Neill, who would be a first cousin
of James McCartan. My brother, Felix, is married to Delia McCartan,
and my other sister is married to P.J. McElroy of the Down team.*

He is not entirely happy with some of the changes in the game
since his playing days.

*The game has changed a lot. I think there's far too much hand-passing:
it's terrible to see fellas running around in circles in the middle of the
field. I liked the Galway style which won the All-Ireland in 1998 —
we've been waiting a long time for something like that. There was*

plenty of catching and kicking, especially from young Michael Donnellan, who put in an exceptional performance.

'The amateur ethos is gone,' he thinks,

because you have the situation where there is money in the game, with club managers being brought in from outside. The problem is that there are a huge amount of people who have given their lives to the association without ever asking for a penny. Teachers, for example, have given a huge amount to the GAA and got nothing in return in financial terms. I think of teachers like Alf Murray, who gave so much. That type of person will disappear if professionalism takes hold.

McKnight looks back on his career with undisguised affection. 'They were the best years of my life,' he says without hesitation. He has warm memories of the many great characters he met through football.

On our team, the late Pat Campbell was a great character. He had a very quick wit and was always slagging fellas. In those days you didn't have the three subs system that you have now — a player could only come off if he was injured, so the only way around that system was to feign injury. One day Pat was 'injured' and taken off. Our right full-back, Gene Morgan, was a very droll character, and he made a crack at Campbell: 'That's the first time I've seen anybody limping off with a sore finger!'

I started off playing junior football at sixteen years of age. At that stage, it was hard to field a team. There was one guy roped in to play for us and he was provided with boots, socks, a jersey and the lot. We were thrashed, and of course when that happens everybody blames everybody else. When unflattering comments were put to our new recruit, his riposte was, 'Well, you can't blame me. I never got near the ball!'

His dream team is as follows:

John O'Leary (Dublin)
Willie Casey (Mayo) Paddy Prendergast (Mayo) Tom O'Hare (Down)
Jim McDonnell (Cavan) John Cronin (Kerry) Sean Quinn (Armagh)
Jack O'Shea (Kerry) Mick O'Connell (Kerry)
Padraic Carney (Mayo) Sean Purcell (Galway) Paddy Doherty (Down)
Kevin Armstrong (Antrim) Sean O'Neill (Down) Kevin Heffernan (Dublin)

JEEPERS KEEPERS

It was a case of so near and yet so far for goalkeeper Willie Nolan when he captained Offaly to a place in the 1961 All-Ireland final. In front of more than 90,000 spectators — a record crowd — his team lost by a solitary point to the reigning champions, Down.

His football career began in national school in Clara, Co. Offaly, and after winning a stack of under-age medals he graduated to the county minors. He made his senior debut for Offaly in 1958, when he came on as a sub for Larry Fox against Laois, and he retained his place from then on. Offaly were improving as a side, but Kerry beat them easily in the 1959 National League semi-final, and they were beaten by Laois in the first round of the Leinster championship that year also. Offaly had more shape the following year, but it needed a catalyst to pull the threads together. Willie Nolan has no doubt about who that was.

> There was no such thing as a manager then, but Peter O'Reilly, who had trained the Dublin team to win the All-Ireland in 1958, fell out with Dublin, and some of our boys asked him to take us on. He loved being given the chance to get back at Dublin.
>
> We met Dublin in the Leinster semi-final in 1960. I had seen them play in the previous round against Longford — they had beaten them by seven goals — and I thought to myself, 'We're rightly bunched.' But with Peter as our figurehead we were really fired up to win the match for him, and we beat them by 3–9 to 0–9. It was one of the biggest thrills of my life.

Offaly were unable to raise their game to quite the same standard in the Leinster final but still scraped a one-point victory over Laois. It was an historic occasion — the county's first Leinster senior title in either football or hurling. Now they met a more experienced Down team in the All-Ireland semi-final. The match turned on a controversial incident, as Nolan recalls.

We were leading by two points with a couple of minutes to go when Jim McCartan got the ball and charged with it towards the goal. Some of our fellas went towards him and the referee gave them a penalty, which Paddy Doherty scored. We got a point to equalise. Mick Dunne was writing for the Irish Press *at the time and in his report the next day he wrote that it shouldn't have been a penalty, it should have been a free out for charging.*

The final score was Down 1–10, Offaly 2–7. Down went on to win the replay by two points and beat Kerry comfortably in the All-Ireland final.

In 1961, another clash with Carlow paved the way for a Leinster semi-final against Kildare. 'Kildare were supposed to be the coming team that year,' Nolan recalls.

Mind you, they've been saying that nearly every year since, and they still haven't come! There was a lot of hype about them, with the result that the game attracted a massive crowd. So many people were let into the ground that the crowd had to be let in on the sideline, and the referee wouldn't start the match until the two captains got the fans to move back a bit more. We got going eventually and beat Kildare to qualify for another Leinster final against Dublin.

A lot of people in Offaly and elsewhere felt that Dublin should not always have home advantage in Leinster finals and that the match should be taken from Croke Park. The powers-that-be agreed, but where did they hold it? Portlaoise. Sure they couldn't get in or get out with the chaos. All hell broke out after the match — and it wasn't too easy during the game either! There wasn't a final played outside Croke Park since.

Whatever the disorder at the game, Offaly accounted for Dublin and then brushed aside the challenge of Roscommon in the All-Ireland semi-final. It was a victory which left Nolan with a tinge of regret.

I was sorry that Gerry O'Malley had to lose that semi-final. He was one of the greatest players. Although he wasn't a stylish player he was very dedicated and had a great heart, and he gave great service to Roscommon.

Nolan led Offaly out on the Croke Park pitch for the final against Down. 'It was the thrill of my life,' he remembers,

but I was as nervous as a kitten. Basically all I had to do [as captain] was keep the backs from roaming up the field. I was lucky I had a great full-back line: Greg Hughes, Johnny Egan and Paddy McCormack. Paddy was a hard man and a great footballer, and went on to win two All-Irelands in 1971 and 1972.

We also had great players up the field. Phil Reilly was a great right half-back. Our centre-back was Mick Brady, father of current Offaly star Peter Brady. He was too classy for that position. He was a much better natural footballer than Jim McCartan, but McCartan was a tough man who could push him out of the way.

Down also succeeded in pushing Offaly's All-Ireland challenge to one side, though at only twenty-one years of age, Willie did not foresee then that his one chance of winning an All-Ireland had passed him by. Although the disappointment of losing the All-Ireland was immense, in 1962 he had the consolation of winning his second consecutive Railway Cup medal, but Offaly surrendered their Leinster title to Dublin in the final that year, in what was to be Nolan's last game with the county.

Losing that match was effectively the end for that Offaly team. My great hero, Mick Casey, had been playing for years and Sean Foran likewise, and we didn't have replacements for them. Offaly won the minor All-Ireland in 1964 and it wasn't until some of those lads came through that Offaly achieved success.

We were invited to America a while after losing the 1962 Leinster final. We played New York twice. My brother, Peter, was playing for them. I stayed on for a few weeks after the tour because I had two brothers over there, and I came back in November. Offaly had played two matches in the league at that stage. The chairman of Offaly County Board was very annoyed with me for staying on in America, and although Peter O'Reilly was supposed to be in charge, the chairman had the final say and there was no way he was going to let me play again. My heart was broken because I wasn't playing football, so I went back to America to stay. I started playing with Offaly in New York. At the time, every county who won the league came out to play New York. In 1963 Dublin came over and we beat them. That was one of the biggest thrills of my life. Four years later we beat the great Galway three-in-a-row side, which was another great thrill.

In 1964, Nolan was drafted into the US army and served in Vietnam. Asked about his memories of his military career, all he says is, 'I don't like to talk about it.' Our conversation takes place in the pub where he works in Ballycumber. The Kosovo crisis is at its height, and as Sky News unfolds more horrifying images on the television screen in the corner, Willie talks sadly as he compares the tragedy in the Balkans with the situation he found himself in in Vietnam.

Nudged towards memories of his playing days, he soon brightens and the recollections that emerge are affectionate, vivid and entertaining. Asked about the greatest player he ever saw, Nolan answers promptly:

Mick O'Connell was the best natural footballer I ever saw because of his sheer ability, class and fitness, although he played on some very average Kerry teams. He had great tussles with Offaly's Willie Bryan in 1972. In the second half of the replay Willie pulled ahead, and in the last twenty minutes he was something special, but I'd love to have seen them clash when they were both at their peak. Willie Bryan was also a great natural footballer, though Sean Purcell was the second-best natural footballer I ever saw.

Nolan has a long list of footballers whom he ranks as great players, though, given the difficulties of comparing players from different eras, he is reluctant to name his dream team.

Down's Sean O'Neill and Paddy Doherty were exceptional forwards, as was Kevin Heffernan. Louth's Stephen White was right up there with the best of them, as was Leitrim's Packy McGarty. Westmeath's Mick Carley was another great player; I won two Railway Cups with him. It was a great competition then because it didn't matter whether you were from a weak county or a strong one — all that mattered was talent, and a good player always stood out because the cream always rose to the top. Mick was more than a match for the star players from Down or Kerry. Wicklow had great players in Gerry O'Reilly and Jim Rogers. Derry's Jim McKeever was something special. He was certainly one of the greatest players never to win an All-Ireland medal.

Who were the players Nolan admired most since he retired?

Colm O'Rourke was a great forward. He could give it and take it. I don't want to talk about my own, but I would have to mention Matt Connor, who was in a league of his own. I was always a great admirer of Martin Furlong too.

Although he has many happy memories from his playing days, Nolan has none of the medals he won as a player.

I don't have any of my medals because I gave them all away to various people over the years. When you're playing it's the winning that matters, not the medals. Only as you got older do the medals start to become important.

O'REILLY: ACE OF FIVES

Jimmy Magee is one of sport's great commentators. The wonder and admiration he feels for sport forges a bond between him and other fans whose only experience of big occasions comes through radio and television. The credibility he enjoys with Irish sports fans is testimony to his skill and integrity as a broadcaster.

His job has given him access to some of sport's most compelling performers. If he were to compile a list of those who thrilled him most, their names would spill over many a page. But alongside Christy Ring, Mick O'Connell and Pele would be a number whose lack of celebrity did not diminish their impact on a match.

When I asked him who were the greatest players never to win All-Ireland medals, he had just one name on his list of hurlers: Clare's Ger Loughnane.

In 1995 I had all my childhood dreams come true when I commentated live on UTV on my first All-Ireland final. I was in absolute heaven. Clare won the match and over the next few years I had a lot of contact with Ger in a professional capacity. I always found him to be incredibly helpful and co-operative and never demanding in any way.

Gerry O'Reilly says he's 'not bad for 73'.

There were a lot more possibilities in the world of football. One name that would probably surprise many people is Tom Spillane, father of the three Spillanes. He won a Railway Cup medal with Munster but was one of the few great Kerry players who never got to play on a winning All-Ireland side. Pat would have to be on any dream team, like a lot of other Kerry players, such as Mike Sheehy. The big problem with such a team would be to select which three Kerry players at midfield: Paddy Kennedy, Jack O'Shea and Mick O'Connell.

I'll always remember playing a match with the Jimmy Magee All-Stars, when my son, who was a handy player, went up for a ball only for Mick O'Connell to soar like an eagle and take it off him. My son said to me afterwards, 'That man is in his fifties. What must he have been like in his prime?'

Having said all of that about Kerry lads, the first man I would have on a team of all-time greats would be Galway's Sean Purcell.

I think the first man on my team of greatest players never to win an All-Ireland would be Louth's Eddie Boyle, especially because of the longevity of his career. He's one of the few men who could have played in any era, with his high catch, great ball-playing skills like John O'Keeffe, and he never fouled. My late father thought the sun shone out of him. He was a full-forward and Eddie was a full-back so they had many a tussle in club football. Two Roscommon players come to mind straight away. I've always been a big admirer of Dermot Earley as a player and as a sportsman, and there's also Gerry O'Malley.

Wicklow have produced some great players who've never won All-Irelands. I was talking to one player in this category, Kevin O'Brien, last year. He is one of the best players in the modern game but because he is with a weaker county in football terms, his year is over after the first game in the championship, which they invariably lose. When I asked him how he coped with the disappointment, he told me that he was involved with some of the Kosovo refugees and compared to what they went through his disappointments in football are inconsequential.

In a previous generation Wicklow had great players as well, like Moses Coffey and Jim Rogers, who was a great midfielder in the old style. Andy Phillips was a great goalkeeper who toyed with soccer for a while; he played for Shelbourne and could have made it cross-channel if he had gone for it.

But very close to the top of any list of great players who never won
an All-Ireland medal was Gerry O'Reilly. He was a sensational wing-
back, but the only time you'd see him play was on St Patrick's Day in
Croke Park, playing for Leinster. That evening people would be saying
what a marvellous player Gerry O'Reilly was and how they'd have to
wait for another year to see him perform again. He was tenacious, a
good kicker, worked hard and never seemed to play badly. The closest
player I've seen to him in modern times was Kerry's Páidí Ó Sé. They
even looked a bit like each other. They both knew that the first job of a
back is to stop a forward from scoring.

Gerry O'Reilly was right half-back on the team of the century
for players who never won All-Ireland medals, and he was one of
the nominees for the team of the millennium. He first came to
prominence as a half-forward with Donard, Co. Wicklow, but he
unexpectedly found himself converted into a half-back in a move
born out of desperation. As things turned out, it was a perfect
switch.

Donard had no minor club at the time so I made my start with the
junior team. I was selected at half-forward for the Wicklow minor
team in 1946 and played there in the Leinster championship. I was a
sub on the senior team the day Wicklow played Carlow in the Leinster
championship. Carlow's Jim Rea was playing ducks and drakes with
the Wicklow defence, and I'll always remember Billy Lawless
instructing me to go on and 'tie up Jim Rea'. I went on and stayed at
right half-back from then on.

Wicklow had a very poor team in the 1940s. Times were pretty
hard then and we had to walk to Donard to get a lift before travelling
with the county team. I remember walking one day with Tony Rogers,
Jim's brother, when it poured out of the heavens. My feet were so
soaked that I had to wear my football boots in the car!

I was a total unknown in the west of Ireland when I made my
debut for Leinster in the Railway Cup against Connacht in 1952. The
only Connacht player who had heard of me was Galway's Tom
McHugh, who played his club football in Wicklow and had played on
me a number of times. Of course, who did I end up marking that day
only Tom McHugh. The game went really well for me so after a while
they switched the great Sean Purcell on to me. Sean did not last very

long because we had a clash of heads, and then they switched Roscommon's Eamon Boland on to me. He was a very big man but the first thing he said to me was, 'You're playing havoc today.'

O'Reilly went on to win four Railway Cup medals. The highpoint of his career, however, came at club level.

My proudest moments were winning my two county medals with Donard, in 1947 and 1957. My big regret was that I didn't win more with them. I played a lot of my club football in Dublin with Guinness's because I was doing shift work and there was no other option. In the 1950s club football was very strong in Dublin with our club, St Vincent's and Sean McDermott's. I often saw inter-provincial players who couldn't get on to the Sean McDermott's team then. The standard of players was so high that playing club football some Sunday mornings was like playing in an All-Ireland.

O'Reilly played inter-county football until 1960, and in the process lined out with some of the greatest players of all time. Who was the greatest of them all?

Over a good number of years, Sean Purcell came closest to being the complete footballer. He was a real all-rounder.

When asked about his most difficult opponent, he responds with a virtual litany.

I played on a lot of top players, such as Jim Rea, Louth's Frankie Byrne, Kevin Heffernan, Sean Purcell and Packy McGarty. The player who gave me the most problems was Meath's Paddy Meegan. He was a very foxy player. I learned a few tricks about how to mark a fella from him.

He selected a Wicklow team-mate when asked about his favourite character in the game.

All the players back then were great characters. My favourite was Kit Carroll from Dunlavin, who played with me on the Wicklow minor team. Like myself, he was fond of a pint after a game. What was unusual about Kit, though, was that after a match he would have an auction at the bar for his socks and jersey and would always get a pound or two!

O'Reilly believes passionately that the 1940s and 1950s were a vintage era for Gaelic football, and is not too impressed by the changes that have taken place in the game.

The standard is nowhere near as high now as it was in our time. In fact, it's a different game now with so much hand-passing. The other huge change is that positional play means nothing. Players now can turn up anywhere. A right half-back can pop up to score a goal.

Now based in Wales, O'Reilly keeps in close touch with the world of Gaelic games.

From time to time I come home for matches. In 1997 I returned for the All-Ireland between Meath and Kerry, when Maurice Fitzgerald won the game for Kerry from play and from frees. It was a real one-man show.

Although he has many happy memories from his playing days, O'Reilly admits also to a few regrets.

We had a great team from 1953 to 1955, with players like Andy Phillips, Joe Timmons and Johnny Timmons. The biggest disappointment of my career came when we played Meath in the Leinster semi-final. We were winning by a point at full-time, but for some reason they played four or five minutes of injury time, and we ended up losing by a point.

While we had players to match anybody, our problem was that we had the worst county board in Ireland. The training was terrible. They had the slowest player on the team out in front when we were running laps: I would always have the fastest guy out in front. Is it any wonder we never won anything?

Captain Marvel

Sue Ramsbottom has gone boldly where no female has gone before. She first made her mark at primary school in Timahoe, Co. Laois, and went on to win a unique Laois under-12 county championship medal playing with the parish boys' team.

I was a tomboy. My brother was a few years older than me, so when they were picking teams at break-time in school I was always on his team. After a while I was picked for the school team; then I was selected for the parish team. I played midfield with Damien Delaney, who plays for Laois now, and also with his brother Eamon. It was no big deal for me because I was training with them anyway.

It may not have been a big issue for Sue, but the traditionalists were not impressed.

It wasn't looked on favourably by some of the teachers and others, but there was nothing my mother could do to stop me playing. I was lucky in that three other girls came on the scene with me — Lulu Carroll, Amanda Donoghue and Niamh McEvoy — and we progressed together through the ranks.

Sue got her first taste of competing in front of a huge crowd contesting the INTO skills competition at the interval during a Leinster football final. Although she got to know Mosney very well, and won multiple medals at the Community Games, her big breakthrough came when she was asked to play with a local club team, the Heath. Her progress was nothing less than spectacular.

They were the best ladies club team in the country then — the
Ballymacarbry of their time. They had some of the giants of the game
on the side, like Kathleen Murphy. I was very lucky insofar as the girls
were very responsible and, for example, never went to the pubs when I
was with them. I was only in fifth class but I won a senior All-Ireland
club medal with them. It didn't mean anything to me at that age
really, but now of course I realise how hard they are to come by. I was
a tall, strong, sturdy eleven year old so I generally was more than able
to hold my own — but I still have the bruises from that match! I scored,
so nothing was going to faze me that day.

I played in my first senior inter-county All-Ireland against Kerry
when I was fourteen. It was the first ladies' football final played in
Croke Park and partly because of that it got great coverage in the local
papers. I scored, so that was a big thrill even though we lost. It's a great
stage and to be playing in an All-Ireland final at fourteen is fabulous. I
got my first All-Star that year too, so that was great.

The teenage years are notorious for their fads, but while most
of Ramsbottom's contemporaries were besotted with the fresh
faces of Jason Donovan and Bros, Sue's two heroes were less likely
pin-up material: Barney Rock and Colm O'Rourke.

I went through a huge phase of being Barney Rock! I used to think I was
him taking frees. I had him off to a T with the seven-steps-back routine.
When Barney retired and Charlie Redmond took his place, I

experimented with his tech-
nique at frees for a while, too.
But when I was playing, I was
Colm O'Rourke. He was the
ultimate footballer. In 1996 I
was chosen as The Sunday
Game's *player of the match for*
the All-Ireland final. It would
have been a great honour for
me in any circumstances, but
what made it one of the
highlights of my career was that
the selection was made by
Colm O'Rourke.

Sue Ramsbottom receives her award
for Player of the Year in 1996.

Sue found herself propelled into the exalted company of top players like O'Rourke and Micky Linden when, in an imaginative effort to increase the profile of Gaelic games among children, the GAA introduced a collection of cards featuring photos of top players, which were distributed with Kellogg's breakfast cereals. Yet despite her admiration for O'Rourke, he has to take second place in Sue's hierarchy of GAA greats.

> One of the most special moments of my life came after one of the All-Irelands when I was approached by Mícheál Ó Muircheartaigh and he drove me out to RTÉ for an interview. Just to be in his company meant an awful lot, but the fact that he went to such trouble for me really made my day.

Given her status within the game, does this not put inordinate pressure on her shoulders when Laois play?

> Laois have produced some of the best players in the history of ladies' football but we still haven't won the All-Ireland. It's a team game. There's no one individual going to win an All-Ireland on her own. You need a squad giving it everything. As you get older you want to win more and more. I've played in seven All-Ireland finals and I've still not won one. Although I've won All-Stars and other awards, the one thing I want to win is an All-Ireland medal. That would be everything to me.
>
> I don't think anybody realises the effort we put in. It starts in February with endurance work, then we work on speed and as we get closer to the championship we focus on ball work. Coming up to the All-Ireland in 1996, we trained at 6.30 in the morning and then again in the evening, with just the odd day off. There was one week when we trained every morning at 6.30 a.m. It's very hard on your social life; there's certainly no drinking while you are in the championship.

When she finished school Ramsbottom joined the army, and after a twenty-one-month stint in cadet school she was transferred to Custume Barracks in Athlone. 'It has a very strong football connection,' she points out.

> One of the first people I saw there was former Mayo great, Kevin McStay. John Maughan had been based there and was an occasional visitor, and a third former Mayo star, Sean Kilbride, was a prominent

figure in the barracks. The army has given a huge amount of talent to Gaelic games down through the years, and that trend is continuing with young players like Dermot Earley in Kildare and Brian Walsh in Sligo.

Sue is a natural athlete. She has won All-Ireland medals in basketball and volleyball and is also an international rugby player.

While I was based in Athlone I did a degree in computers in University College Galway, so I started playing rugby for Galwegians to give myself something to do for the winter. Then I was selected to play in the inter-provincials and after that I was asked if I would take part in an Irish trial. I did and went on to win three caps against England, Scotland and Wales. Unfortunately, I had to miss out on the World Cup in Holland in 1998 because it came immediately before my final exams. I was a kicking full-back. Any time I saw a big one charging at me, I got rid of it as fast as I could!

After graduating from the army cadet school, in autumn 1998 Ramsbottom began a six-month tour of duty with the Irish Army's UN mission in the Lebanon.

'It was a great experience, though there were a few "incidents,"' she says matter of factly.

I was lucky in that my turn came in the winter so I did not lose out in football terms. There was plenty of sports people in our group like the former Limerick hurler, Pat Herbert, and usually there were plenty of opportunities for training, except when there was heavy shelling. Twice a week I would run ten kilometres and most other days I would run two or three miles. We also had a football and I got to know it very well!

Ramsbottom's departure for the Lebanon coincided with a controversy in Roscommon over VEC member Malachy Byrne's opposition to a £900 grant allocated by Roscommon VEC for the promotion of ladies' football. The controversy was fuelled further when he sought to explain himself on Shannonside radio, saying,

I reckon that a lady's or girl's body is too precious to be abused, bumped and humped playing football. Their bodies are not made for humps and bumps. They have their own natural humps and bumps.

Given the prevalence of this type of attitude, is it not surprising that the vast majority of coaches in ladies' football are men?

You need a strong character to manage a team and most men learn to adapt. Our club coach, for example, is Pat Critchley, who trained the Carlow men's team, and he knows that you have to modify your style a bit when coaching ladies. But many of the principles are the same, like knowing how to coach different players in different ways: some need to have the pressure put on them; others need lots of encouragement. Some things, though, that might work well with men don't work as well with women.

I think back to one of our All-Ireland finals. We were losing at half-time and when we got back to the dressing-room one of our mentors, who is a lovely, considerate woman, said, 'I've put the kettle on and we'll have a cup of tea.' Our manager immediately thumped the table ferociously and everything on it went flying all over the place. Then he yelled (in less polite language), 'How the hell could you think of tea at a time like this?' To be honest, I find that kind of thumping on the desk approach more funny than inspirational.

I do think it's time for us to have more female coaches. Westmeath have appointed the former Waterford player, Marie Crotty, as their coach, and she seems to be doing great work.

Although she is still only in her mid-twenties, would Sue consider a coaching career when her playing days are over?

Give me some men's county team and I'd get them into shape. There'd be some shock, wouldn't there? Pat Spillane would have something to say then!

How would Sue like to see the game marketed?

People like Helen O'Rourke are doing a great job on that front. We have so many great players in the game and I think they are the best promotion for it. To take one example, Maurice Fitzgerald's sister is a star player. She is so like Maurice on the ball it's unreal. She never seems to be moving fast, but it's very hard to keep up with her!

Given her role as a captain in the army, Sue is curtailed from campaigning on political issues, but she put all such restraints aside to align herself publicly with the 'Free the Laois One' campaign.

After we lost our last All-Ireland we were really devastated; everyone was absolutely heartbroken. There was a big hype at home before the game, and they painted a Beetle in the Laois colours, blue and white, put all our names on it, and parked the car as near as possible to Croke Park on the day of the match. The next morning, we heard the car was missing. It had been impounded because there was no tax on it — the car was so old there was no point in paying tax on it for the day, though it was insured. We were staying in a hotel in Lucan but we decided to go into town to rally outside the police station and try and get the car back. One of the biggest characters in our team, Lulu Carroll, made up a song which we all chanted:

Where's the Beetle gone?
Far, far away
The cops took it away.

It must have looked a funny sight to have seen all these women singing outside the cop shop! We thought our song would get the car free, but no such luck. It became a big media story and was discussed on Marian Finucane's show, and eventually the saga was resolved when a professor from Trinity College volunteered to pay the £100 fine and the car was released.

Selecting the dream team she would like to play on produced many agonising choices for her, but eventually Sue Ramsbottom settled on the following:

Teresa Swayne (Laois)
Máiréad Kelly (Monaghan) Martina O'Ryan (Waterford) Noreen Walsh (Waterford)
Katie Liston (Kerry) Jenny Greenan (Monaghan) Margaret Phelan (Laois)
Mary Jo Curran (Kerry) Kathleen Murphy (Laois)
Angela Larkin (Monaghan) Sue Ramsbottom (Laois) Catriona Casey (Waterford)
Geraldine O'Ryan (Waterford) Áine Wall (Waterford) Edel Byrne (Monaghan)

PRIDE AND PASSION

Meath football has always been a place where the weak don't survive. Hence a club secretary's report which recorded,

_____ _____ *made his championship debut in such a way that he will never be asked to make it again!*

Ken Rennicks was one player who consistently displayed the pride and passion that characterises the men who wear the green and gold of Meath. After playing for the county minor team, he made his senior inter-county debut in a game against Offaly in 1969. The following year he scored three points in one of the most exciting and dramatic provincial football finals of all time, which Meath, after trailing by eleven points, won by 2–22 to 5–12. The high of such a win was followed by bitter disappointment when the Royal County lost the All-Ireland final to a Kerry team captained by Donie O'Sullivan. The match saw the coming of age of a young man who would go on to become one of the immortals of the game, nineteen-year-old John O'Keeffe, who gave a commanding performance at centre half-back on the great Matt Kerrigan. The game was the last hurrah for the great Meath team that Peter Darby had captained to All-Ireland glory in 1967. Younger players like Rennicks could not have foreseen that Meath would have to wait until 1986 to win another Leinster final.

In 1974 Rennicks won a Railway Cup medal with Leinster, the province's first title for twelve years, and the following season Meath won a National League title with a great victory over reigning All-Ireland champions Dublin. Rennicks ranks that match as his greatest game. The icing on the cake came in the shape of an All-Star award, 'the biggest honour I could receive in my career.'

In the mid-1970s, however, seismic shifts were taking place in the football landscape, and counties like Meath were struggling to maintain a foothold. Dublin and Kerry were pioneering a revolution, introducing a more professional and innovative approach to the game. How did Rennicks evaluate Heffo's army?

There were one of the best teams I have seen, always very well prepared and very skilful. Sometimes it got very disappointing after they arrived, because we were out of the championship so early. If we were longer in it, we would have been better prepared to take on a side that good.

As if the great Dublin team was not sufficiently formidable opposition for Rennicks's Meath, along came an even more fearsome Kerry side. In addition to their exceptional skills and fitness, Rennicks was a big admirer of their intelligent approach to the game. Former Dublin great, Gay O'Driscoll, has an anecdote which illustrates this point perfectly.

I marked Mike Sheehy in his first match for Kerry in Killarney, when he was picked at top of the left. He never played on me again. Before we played Kerry in a league final, Kevin Heffernan reminded me about that and encouraged me to renew my acquaintance with Mike. I went

in on him early in the game with a hard shoulder and knocked him over, and a free was given against me. As Mike pulled himself up, he said, 'Ah shit, Gay, that's not your game.' It completely took the wind out of my sails. It was a brilliant piece of psychology on his part.

After he retired from football, Rennicks became involved in coaching young players with his native club, Bohermeen, now known as St Ultan's. He looks back on his long association with the club with a glow of satisfaction.

Ken Rennicks poses for the camera.

Bohermeen won the junior championship in the mid-1960s and I started playing with the club when we were an intermediate team. For three or four years we were always in the shake-up of the championship but failed to get the breakthrough. Eventually our time came, and in 1974 we went the whole way to the senior final. We were beaten in the final by a point. The next year we joined up with another team in the parish called Martry and the name of team became Bohermeen Martry Harps. That year we got to the semi-final of the senior championship, and again we lost by a point. Shortly after that the team broke up and some of the players went back to Bohermeen. I stood on with the existing team and we went intermediate. I coached them to a county championship victory in 1975.

Offered the job of selecting a dream team, Rennicks's line out is:

John O'Leary (Dublin)

Gay O'Driscoll (Dublin) Darren Fay (Meath) Donie O'Sullivan (Kerry)

Tommy Drumm (Dublin) John O'Keeffe (Kerry) Martin O'Connell (Meath)

John McDermott (Meath) Mick O'Connell (Kerry)

Maurice Fitzgerald (Kerry) Colm McAlarney (Down) Tony McTague (Offaly)

Colm O'Rourke (Meath) Sean O'Neill (Down) John Egan (Kerry)

IN THE LINE OF DUTY

Of all the matches I have attended, the one most vivid in my memory is the Connacht final of 1980, when two opposing teams were united in grief for a favourite son, John Morley, one of the greatest footballers never to win an All-Ireland medal.

Garda John Morley was murdered just a few days before the Connacht final, on 7 July 1980, with a fellow native of Knock, Henry Byrne. Another Mayo man and centre-forward for Michael Glavey's GAA club, Derek Kelly, was injured in the incident when their squad car encountered a getaway car after a robbery thought to have been carried out by republican activists. Shots were fired and Henry Byrne and John Morley were fatally wounded.

John had initially been based in Ballaghadereen on the Mayo-Roscommon border. He moved to Roscommon town and finally to Castlerea. In all three places he had immersed himself in all manner of community activities.

The violent tragedy of his death had a huge effect in Connacht. The Connacht final was to be played on the following Sunday, between Mayo — a county John had played for for many years — and Roscommon, the county in which he lived and

John Morley, near right, with the Connacht trophy, 1967.

worked. Everybody in both counties respected him, and admired his prowess as a footballer.

It has become a cliché for journalists and broadcasters to refer to a particular player's 'cultured left foot'. Yet every cliché has a kernel of truth, and from the days when he first sprang to prominence with St Jarlath's College, Tuam, where he won All-Ireland Colleges senior medals in 1960 and 1961, there was never any doubt that John Morley's left foot merited this soubriquet.

His reputation was made once he made his first appearance in the Mayo colours in Charlestown in 1961. His former team-mate, Willie McGee, recalls:

John was always getting slagged about his right leg, but he defended it by saying that without it he couldn't use his left!

John's versatility was such that he could play in almost any position, though for Mayo he played mostly at centre-back. He captained Mayo to their first Connacht senior title for twelve years in 1967, and starred in the 1969 winning side. He stood at the heart of the defence and wore the mantle of captain with implacable authority, and played a then record 112 senior games for the county until his retirement in 1974. He also played a number of games in midfield, notably inspiring Mayo to a second-half comeback against a Galway side apparently cruising to victory in the 1973 Connacht final. His goal was one of the highlights in a powerhouse performance, and only time prevented Mayo from wiping out the arrears as they lost 1–17 to 2–12.

In 1975, when Mayo lost to Sligo in the Connacht final replay, Mayo's Sean Kilbride attributed their defeat to the absence of John Morley, specifically the failure of the powers-that-be to lure him out of retirement. Kilbride felt that Morley's experience was the missing link in what was potentially a very good Mayo team.

One of the more renowned incidents in his illustrious career came in the 1970 League final clash in which Mayo defeated Down. Morley was playing at centre half-back, when a Down player grabbed him and tore his shorts. Just as he was about to put on a new pair the ball came towards him; Morley abandoned his sports wear, and in his briefs fielded the ball and cleared it down the field. The crowd rose in applause.

Former Roscommon great, Dermot Earley, frequently came up against Morley, but his outstanding memory of him is of a match they played together for Connacht.

After winning the Railway Cup in 1969, we went out to New York to play in the Cardinal Cushing games. In our first game against New York, I was playing very well in midfield, and on one occasion I jumped to catch a ball hanging in the air. I went into the clouds, or so I thought, but the moment I touched the ball it was taken from my hands. As I reached the ground, I turned quickly to be on the defensive, but I looked around to see that it was John with the ball tucked in as tight as could be, ready to set up another attack.

You would have to consider him as being one of the great players. In the west of Ireland we generally refer to people we admire, even though we may never have met them, by their surname. If you go into any GAA setting in the west of Ireland today and you say 'Morley', everyone will know the name. He remains known by that name with affection and admiration.

Any discussion of John Morley's career is overshadowed by the tragic circumstances of his death. The man who gave every ounce of energy on the playing-field for Mayo was prepared also to put his life on the line to honour his professional duty and uphold law and order. The bravery which he had so often exhibited in the green and red jersey was to manifest itself even more in the dark blue uniform of the Gardaí. A hero in life became a hero in death.

A retired Garda, the late Garda Kneafsey, was first on the scene after the clash between Gardaí and bank robbers, and found John Morley on the side of the road, bleeding badly. He recognised 'the footballer' and bent over him to give him aid. 'I'm getting awful cold,' Morley told Kneafsey. Then he said an Act of Contrition. Shortly afterwards the ambulance arrived, but it was too late to save John.

The priest found it difficult to preach the funeral homily. Saying 'the few words' seemed so inadequate. Crucifixion and resurrection do not find ready echoes in the life of young children who have just lost a father. There were no simple answers to the questions overshadowing the congregation's prayers.

The Connacht final was played on Sunday 13 July, a day of brilliant summer sun, and before the throw-in Fr Leo Morahan of the Connacht Council gave a poignant oration in memory of a great man and a superb footballer. In the circumstances, Roscommon's 3-13 to 0-8 win hardly seemed to matter.

John Morley's spirit lives on in Mayo football through the fine performances of his son, Gordon.

In 1997 John was chosen at centre-back on the *Western People*'s best Mayo team 1960-1990. The team in full was as follows:

Eugene Rooney

Willie Casey   Ray Prendergast   Dermot Flanagan

Johnny Carey   John Morley   Eamon Walsh

Willie Joe Padden   T.J. Kilgallon

Joe Langan   John Gibbons   Joe Corcoran

Martin Carney   Willie McGee   J.J. Cribbins

APPENDICES

I
WIRED FOR SOUND

Writer and broadcaster Mick Dunne is one of the unsung heroes of the GAA, having served twenty-one years as Gaelic games correspondent with the *Irish Press* and an equal number with RTÉ. Dunne had originally decided to study for the priesthood, but after a year and a half in All Hallows seminary he decided that the clerical life was not for him. There was a considerable stigma attached to being a 'spoiled priest' at that time, but his family supported his decision fully.

The Tailor Dunnes, as Mick's family was known due to the number in the clan who took up tailoring, lived at the foot of the Slieve Bloom mountains in Clonaslee, Co. Laois. His father, Frank, commanded the Laois 4th Battalion of the IRA in the War of Independence, and during the Civil War spent forty-four days on hunger strike in Mountjoy prison. His cell was on the same landing as future Taoiseach Sean Lemass and Sean Coughlan, who subsequently became the GAA columnist with the *Irish Press*, writing under the pen name 'Green Flag'.

Coughlan was young Mick Dunne's hero, and when he came back from matches with his father on Sundays he would take out his copybook and write reports of the game he had just watched,

Mick Dunne enjoys a quiet moment.

signing himself 'Green Flag'. He followed in his idol's footsteps, joining the *Irish Press* as junior librarian in 1949 and becoming Gaelic games correspondent and then Gaelic games editor the following year. His rapid progress was not without its awkward moments.

I once sat in a hotel having my breakfast the morning after a Munster final and two tables away I could hear two men dissecting my report on the match. Their remarks weren't very complimentary! Another incident that I recall from those days came when I had a bit of trouble with my editor because when I wrote my reports about Kilkenny matches I always spoke of the 'Diamond' Hayden. The editor hated us using pet names and read me the riot act. I pointed out that if you went down to Kilkenny and asked anybody what the Diamond's Christian name was, no one would be able to tell you. He was known as the 'Diamond' and by nothing else. The editor conceded the argument and I continued to write about the 'Diamond'.

Had he been alive today, Westmeath's 'Jobber' McGrath, chosen at midfield on the centenary team of players who never won an All-Ireland hurling medal, would have been a must for this book. Mick Dunne tells the inside story of how the Jobber got his nickname.

My wife's twin brother, Joe Fox, actually christened him 'Jobber'. When they went to school as young lads, Joe couldn't say Johnny properly so he called him 'Jobba', and that's where the name came from.

In 1970 Dunne was headhunted by Mícheál O'Hehir to strengthen RTÉ's coverage of Gaelic games. He made his debut as a commentator in handball with the popular *Top Ace* series.

'Commentating,' he says, 'is the nearest thing to playing because you get caught up in the game.'

You're living on adrenaline. Of course, sometimes things go wrong. One day I was commentating in Thurles when my monitor tipped over and fell into the crowd. I had to carry on commentating and at the same time retrieve the monitor, which I can tell you wasn't very good for the blood pressure!

Of all the games he commentated on, one gave him particular pleasure.

It was when Laois won the National Football League in 1986. It was the first time in sixty years for Laois to win a national competition and I was euphoric, though unlike the fans I could not show it. I met a friend from Cork the following day and he said to me, 'You know, boy, you'd never think you were a Laois man listening to your commentary,' which I thought was a great compliment.

One of the privileges of his career was to meet with some of the great personalities of Gaelic games. 'Nicky Rackard was one of the most colourful characters I ever met,' he recalls.

He changed the whole sporting and social structure of Wexford. He went to St Kieran's College in Kilkenny and developed a love for hurling which he brought home to his brothers and to his club, Rathnure. Wexford had traditionally been a football power, going back to their famous four-in-a-row side. But Nicky Rackard turned Wexford into a recognised hurling bastion almost overnight. It was a tragedy that he died so young. As people know, he had his problems with the drink, but at his funeral I spoke to his brother Bobby, who told me it was a great shame he died because he had been doing great work for AA at the time.

The famous John Kerry O'Donnell of New York was a wonderful character. Back in the 1960s I was involved with other Gaelic games journalists in selecting the team that would travel to New York to play in the Cardinal Cushing games to raise money for the Cardinal's mission in Peru. It was almost the precursor of the All-Stars. We tried especially to pick some good players from the weaker counties, and in fact the former GAA president, John Dowling, always maintained that one of the reasons why Offaly eventually made the breakthrough in hurling was because of the boost it got when players like Paddy Molloy got on one of these trips.

John Kerry dined out for years in America on the story of what happened when this gang of Irish journalists got together. The importance of picking players from the weaker counties led us to speak about the terms of reference in selection decisions. However, at that one of our number blurted out, 'Let's pick the team first and we'll sort out the terms of reference later!'

Later, Dunne was for many years secretary to the journalists who selected the All-Stars. The fruit of their deliberations often generated controversy, for their perceived sins of omission as much as their actual selection. Selecting the best fifteen provoked passionate disagreements among the journalists in question. Mick recalls that,

When he was president of the GAA, after seeing us picking the teams, Pat Fanning remarked, 'The amazing thing is that they are such good friends after a night arguing like this!'

The president and director general of the GAA sat in as observers. The only time they ever intervened was if there was a tie over a particular position. Having listened to all the arguments, then they went out of the room and decided who got the nod.

Controversy erupted in 1985 when Paul Earley was chosen at full-forward on the All-Star football team ahead of Monaghan's Eamonn

Murphy. A prominent GAA personality in Monaghan subsequently wrote an article which claimed that Earley was awarded the honour because he was an employee of the sponsoring bank. Dunne rejects the suggestion outright.

The accusation that the bank interfered in Paul's selection was totally wrong and very unfair to his abilities as a player. If they had tried to persuade us to pick Paul, it would have ensured that he wouldn't get the All-Star!

The only time I ever got 'approached' was when I got a phone-call from a manager the day before the team was picked. After a bit of casual conversation he blatantly started talking up some of his players with a view to influencing my selection. I simply said, 'It would be much better for their chances if you didn't interfere in this way.'

Some players stand above all argument, and when I asked Mick Dunne who the greatest hurler he ever saw was, he answered immediately: 'Christy Ring.'

Without question he was the greatest player I ever saw. He was probably the greatest player that ever laced a boot. He was the one I admired most, the man I was most happy to report upon and the man I was always pleased to talk with, although like many another hurling or football genius he wasn't always very approachable.

When asked about the greatest footballer he ever saw, the answer is equally emphatic.

Galway's Sean Purcell was the best. It could be said that there were better players in different positions but as far as I'm concerned he was the best all-round footballer. I remember him at full-back in the Connacht semi-final in 1954 against Mayo. It was one of the finest individual displays I've ever seen. He played on the great Tom Langan, then Danny Neill and then John Nallen, but it was all the same, Purcell was superb. He was also a magnificent midfielder and, as a centre-forward, the brains of the Galway team that won the All-Ireland in 1956. He had such a wonderful combination with the other Galway maestro, Frankie Stockwell.

Since his retirement from RTÉ Sport in 1991, Dunne broadcasts occasionally and devotes much of his time to writing. Apart from assisting the late Mícheál O'Hehir as co-writer of the great commentator's life story, Mick wrote *The Star Spangled Final* in 1997 to commemorate the 50th anniversary of the All-Ireland football final played in New York in 1947, and produced *Playing with the Guards*, a history of the Garda GAA Club, in 1998. He is a member of two Irish Handball Council sub-committees and helps that body with public relations.

Asked to select his dream teams, he was so spoilt for choice from all the great players he has reported on that he requested a special dispensation to pick his top twenty instead, and the greatest handballers he has watched too.

Hurling: Noel Skehan (Kilkenny), Ger Cunningham (Cork), Bobbie Rackard (Wexford), Pat Henderson (Kilkenny), John Doyle (Tipperary), Joe Hennessy (Kilkenny), Tony Wall (Tipperary), Pat Stakelum (Tipperary), Willie O'Connor (Kilkenny), Joe Salmon (Galway), Mick Roche (Tipperary), Christy Ring (Cork), Joe Cooney (Galway), Eddie Keher (Kilkenny), Jimmy Langton (Kilkenny), Ray Cummins (Cork), Jimmy Smyth (Clare), Frankie Walsh (Waterford), Jimmy Doyle (Tipperary) and D.J. Carey (Kilkenny)

Football: Billy Morgan (Cork), Johnny Geraghty (Galway), Enda Colleran (Galway), Jerome O'Shea (Kerry), Noel Tierney (Galway), Paddy Prendergast (Mayo), Sean Flanagan (Mayo), Gerry O'Malley (Roscommon), Martin O'Connell (Meath), Jack O'Shea (Kerry), Mick O'Connell (Kerry), Brian Mullins (Dublin), Jimmy Foley (New York), Sean Purcell (Galway), Packy McGarty (Leitrim), Mícheál Kearins (Sligo), Mike Sheehy (Kerry), Sean O'Neill (Down), Kevin Heffernan (Dublin) and John Egan (Kerry)

Top Five Handballers: Pat Kirby (Clare), Duxie Walsh (Kilkenny), Naty Alverado (Mexico), David Chapman (USA) and Joey Maher (Louth)

2
LEST WE FORGET

As a boy Aidan McAnespie dreamed of becoming one of the great Tyrone footballers. Like many youngsters, though, his talent did not match his aspirations. The running joke in the McAnespie family was that the only way an All-Ireland medal would come into their home was if one of them married an All-Ireland winner! In fact that prophecy came true when Aidan's sister-in-law, Brenda, won two All-Ireland medals with the Monaghan ladies football team.

On the playing fields Aidan's main contribution to his club, Aghaloo, was with the junior team. The closest he normally came to the senior team was watching them from the subs bench or making an occasional appearance in the last few minutes of a match. Yet football and the club dominated his life — until 21 February 1988, when Aidan was shot dead by a British soldier as he went to watch his beloved Aghaloo.

Aidan is not the only member of the GAA to die in the Troubles. Sean Brown from Bellaghy was murdered for apparently no other reason than that he was chairman of a high-profile club. And there have been others.

Aidan's sister, Eilish McCabe, is now the best-known opponent of the removal of the GAA's Rule 21, which bars members of the British security forces from taking part in Gaelic games. Yet in her early childhood, Eilish recalls, the Troubles never really affected her family.

We were all born in a street in the middle of the town. There were six of us. I was the second oldest and the eldest girl. We had a lot of fun, and before 1969 life was very peaceful. My mum was from County Monaghan, just a mile from Aughnacloy. Although the border was very near we were never aware of it until the Troubles began, when the soldiers came on the street.

I remember the anger at the closing of the border roads. Previous to the Troubles it was the smugglers who had been mainly concerned with the border and the customs. When I was a young girl an uncle brought me to Monaghan one day, and I asked him, 'Could I jump the border?' That was a phrase I had heard from adult conversation and in my innocence I thought it sounded great craic to be literally jumping the border!

Things changed very quickly shortly after that. We had a British army checkpoint at the bottom of the town. One Saturday evening there was bedlam outside our house, with people hooting their cars and shouting. I recall asking my mum what had happened and she told me that the crowd had opened one of the border roads and people were trucking across the border.

As a Catholic girl in a mainly Protestant town I was very aware of the fact that from an early age I was different from most other girls in the town. I remember as far back as making my first Holy Communion and walking with my family to the chapel at the top of the town, dressed in my white veil and dress, and the Protestant girls looking at me in bewilderment. I was very aware of my identity.

It was Aidan, though, who would suffer most because of his identity.

We were a very close, tight-knit family, and Aidan was always seen as a baby. As the eldest girl I felt I had a duty to mollycoddle him a little bit, though he sometimes rebelled against that.

Aidan was the youngest member of the family, the only one living at home. He got a job in Monaghan as a poultry processor in the chicken factory, and he travelled up and down every morning and evening. He got a lot of harassment at the border checkpoint from the British soldiers. He made complaints to the army, his trade union, to the parish priest, and through his own solicitor. A year before his death, one national newspaper featured an article on him under the headline: 'Is this the most harassed man in Ireland?' Aidan had gone to the media at the time in the hope of embarrassing the security forces for a while, and it would have worked to some extent in the short term.

What form did this harassment take?

It took different forms. As he drove to work they might just pull him over to the side of the road and keep him there for five minutes; on other occasions they might search his car, maybe take out his lunch-box and search it

The last photo taken of Aidan McAnespie, at the Aghaloo O'Neills Annual Dinner Dance.

with their bare hands and say, 'Enjoy your lunch today, Mac.' They sometimes called him Mac. On his way back they might keep him fifteen or twenty minutes on the side of the road, or ask him where he was coming from or going to, or they might pull him into the big shed and take his car apart. But I think the biggest problem was the fear of the unknown: he was never sure of what was coming next. The only thing that was certain was that they were going to hassle him. He was never going to be in a car that was waved through.

Was he physically assaulted?

On some occasions he was. The most recent one prior to his shooting came one evening as he was coming through the checkpoint on his way home from work. It was raining pretty heavily and the soldiers told him to get out of his car and take off his jacket, which he did. Then they asked him to take off his shoes and socks and he said, 'I can't do that. It's pouring rain.' They pounced on him and threw him down on the road and removed his shoes and socks. He came up to me that night and there were marks around his face and neck. I said we were going to have to make a formal complaint. He didn't want to go down to the police station on his own so my husband went down with him. About six months later he received a letter which said that no disciplinary action would be taken against any member of the security forces.

Dealing with death is always difficult and the suddenness of a violent death is almost impossible to accept. More sadly still, Aidan had just left a family wake shortly before he himself met his death.

That weekend we had a death in the family — my aunt's husband had died from a long-term illness. He was buried on the Sunday morning and all the family were together. We all went back to my aunt's house for a meal and afterwards Aidan got up from the table and said to me, 'I'm away on to see the football match.' He went to the family home and lit the stove so the house would be warm when my mum and dad returned home. He walked 269 yards through the checkpoint when a single shot rang out. Aidan died instantly.

We were still at my aunt's house and I was chatting away with cousins I hadn't seen for a long time. Then my husband came inside and said to me, 'Eilish, I need to speak to you immediately.' I knew from the tone of his voice that it was quite serious but I thought it was just that our kids had been misbehaving. When I went out he said, 'There's been an accident at the checkpoint and I think Aidan's been involved. It's serious.'

We got into the car and drove down, and as we approached the football field I could see an ambulance in the background and I thought to myself, 'I'm on time and I'm going to make it with Aidan to the hospital.' I still wasn't sure what had taken place. I could see a body lying on the ground with a blanket over it, but I didn't believe it was Aidan because the body looked small. I went over towards it and pulled back the blanket. It was Aidan, and he was dead. I held his hand and his hands were very, very warm and I hugged him and embraced him. The crowd all stood in complete silence and I heard my parents coming through. An anger went through my body and left again as the grief came back. When I saw my parents going to witness Aidan on the roadside, that was just unbearable. I couldn't even bear to look at them with Aidan lying there like that.

Aidan had relaxed his hold on life; a harmless young man, come to harm. Eilish began to scream.

The ambulance came and Aidan was put in a body bag and put sitting up in the ambulance, and Dad and I said we were going with him because we couldn't let Aidan go on his own. We sat in the ambulance in total shock all the way to the morgue in Craigavon; that's probably one of the longest journeys I'll ever have in my life. It was a sunny day even though it was February, and as we drove through Armagh children were out playing and people were going on with living, and you just said to yourself, 'This can't be happening.'

It was a long night. We were told around ten o'clock that Aidan's body was going to be returned that night. The doctor had decided that Mum, who had stayed up all night the previous two nights with my aunt, should be sedated, and when I realised Aidan was being brought back to the house I tried to wake her, but I couldn't. We sat up all night, and around six o'clock I was making tea for all the people who stayed up with me when I heard a terrible crying and howling. My mum had woken up from her sleep in a daze and she was standing in the hall looking in at Aidan's room. Aidan was laid out in his new suit in the coffin, with the candles all lit. Mum had woken up in a nightmare — I suppose she had thought it was a nightmare, but the reality of the situation hit her. It is hard when you are going through a situation like that, but when you see your parents going through it it is unbearable.

The emotional trauma for the family was compounded by rumours about the circumstances of Aidan's death and the growing realisation that if they were to extract answers to all their questions drastic measures would be needed.

On the Monday we heard that the soldier who had shot him had claimed he was cleaning his gun and his finger slipped. That evening we decided we weren't happy with the explanation, and nobody from the security forces had come to our door with any comment, so I contacted our solicitor.

I also contacted our doctor to see if he could carry out an autopsy on Aidan's body. Then the Irish government made a statement that they were going to carry out an investigation. We decided then that we would go ahead with the funeral, knowing that there would probably have to be an exhumation of Aidan's body.

It was very tough to see Aidan's body leaving the house on a cold February morning. It was hard to believe the amount of people who were there at the funeral from all parts of Ireland, and I mean all parts. When we walked in we didn't realise that the cardinal was going to be there saying the Mass or that Mick Loftus, president of the GAA, was going to be there, and there were many representatives from the Ulster Council. All the support helped us in a small way to carry our cross.

On the following Saturday we got a phone-call from the Irish government saying that we had permission to have the body exhumed the following morning and brought to Monaghan hospital, with the state pathologist, Dr Harbison, in attendance. The news was a relief to me because I knew an injustice had been done to our family and I had no confidence in British justice, so I believed that the autopsy was an opportunity for us to get to the truth. I remember breaking the news to my mother, and I could see in her eyes that it was taking a lot out of her, but I knew she too wanted to get to the bottom of it. On the Wednesday of that week, a soldier was charged with the unlawful killing of Aidan, but we had no confidence that he was going to be convicted so we knew the onus was on us to get an investigation.

On the Sunday night, when the police had finished with all their forensics, the road was re-opened. Then someone came in and told me that the Monaghan road had been closed again. This made us even more suspicious and later that night someone told me that they had a light on and there was a red mark on the road where Aidan's body was. I wasn't quite aware of what was going on and we were told that three shots went off where they were re-marking the road. The media covered the story but the next day the police came back and said, no, they had been shot at and returned fire. Everyone in the locality denied that shots were fired at them.

The family's pain was exacerbated by the British media's portrayal of Aidan.

The phrase they consistently used to describe Aidan was 'Sinn Féin activist'. That was very hurtful to our family. Aidan was a member of the GAA but had never been involved in any political party or political activity. I myself had stood for Sinn Féin at a local government election in 1985. Aidan had gone out and put up posters for me as a brother would do for a sister, but neither of us had been involved in any political activity since then. I don't think it's right to treat any person the way Aidan was treated, regardless of their political views, but it hurt more to see him portrayed in this way to justify to people in England what the soldier had done.

For Eilish the tyranny of the past can be broken only when they know the truth about their brother's death.

We can't lay our loved one to rest until we know the truth and we get answers. We want to know why this happened. We want to know why there wasn't more done. When Aidan was killed we were handed a life sentence. It's something we have to live with every day of our lives.

The soldier who was charged with Aidan's unlawful killing was never convicted. He'd only spent three months in jail and then he was released and allowed to go home on holiday to his parents because they were having a difficult time coming to visit him but there wasn't any consideration shown to my parents for the difficult time they were having. The soldier was never convicted. We never had him in the witness box, or had the opportunity to have our lawyers cross-examine him. An inquest didn't take place until five years after Aidan's death. A British soldier had been compelled to give evidence, and then we were told on the morning of the inquest that he had gone absent without leave. We still haven't had answers.

'I'm not sure if I'm still angry,' Eilish McCabe says,

but I do feel a great injustice was done to Aidan and until we get at the truth I don't think Aidan will ever be able to rest in peace. I'd love to be able to say we can close the file. There's an anger that a British soldier can shoot somebody and not be accountable for it.

The first thing I noticed when I visited Eilish's home in Aughnacloy was the photo of a smiling Aidan. He is the ghost that will always be with her. The passing of thirteen years has done little to heal her pain.

It's been very difficult. Aidan has been an absent figure from all the family events we've had since, like my brother's wedding. You don't ever forget him. You wonder would he be married now and have children. We are all getting older, but to us Aidan will always be twenty-three.

Aidan's name lives on in a Boston football club. Powered by players from Tyrone, Meath, Mayo, Donegal and Cork, the Aidan McAnespie club had its finest hour in 1998 when it won the All-American Cup, having previously won the New England Cup, and after Christmas every year the players get together to play a challenge match in his memory. A major factor in the club's successes has been the involvement of the great Peter Canavan, unquestionably the greatest current player never to have won an All-Ireland medal.

3
It Could Happen to a Bishop

Despite his long association with Clare hurling, Bishop Willie Walsh is in fact a Tipperary man. Born in the parish of Roscrea, his interest in hurling was stimulated by Tipp's All-Ireland triumph in 1945, which heralded the start of a long era of success for his native county. Walsh's association with Clare began when he went to St Flannan's College in Ennis, at a time when Jimmy Smyth was the uncrowned king of this hurling nursery, and though he never quite made it to the Harty Cup team, he hurled with the school's junior side. His hurling career continued in the seminary at Maynooth College, but came to an abrupt halt after his ordination when he was sent to Rome.

Fr Willie Walsh returned to Ireland in the 1960s and took up a position teaching in St Flannan's, where he immediately became involved in coaching hurling teams. A holy hurling trinity was formed as he worked closely with Fr Seamus Gardiner — a prominent member of the Munster Council for many years — and Fr Hugh O'Dowd. Flannan's had been going through a lean period since the late 1950s, but in 1976 the college won the Harty Cup, the first of five All-Irelands under Fr Willie's stewardship.

In his twenty-five years' coaching with Flannan's, Walsh nurtured the talents of players like Joe MacKenna, Sean Stack, Jim Power, Gerry McInerney, Davie Fitzgerald, Jamesie O'Connor, Anthony Daly, Cyril Lyons, Fergie Tuohy and Conor Clancy. Did he know that each one was a star in the making?

I can certainly recall the first time I saw Jamsie O'Connor play. He was in first year and playing in an under-fifteen match. I saw this very small fella playing at wing-back, and straight away I asked who he was because he looked a real natural.

Other players can look very promising as youngsters but for a variety of reasons don't fulfil their promise. I think straight away of Pat Heffernan, who played for a few years at full-forward with Limerick. He was one of the best centre-backs we ever had at Flannan's, but he got a terrible bad break of the leg when he was at university and never really became the giant of the game we expected.

I would see it as one of the tragedies of the game that Barry Smythe, who is the son of Tim Smythe — who was a world cross-country runner of the 1930s — was just coming to his prime at the age of twenty-two when he sustained a bad back injury. If he hadn't been injured, I've no doubt that he'd have gone on to become one of the great centre-backs of the game, like Sean McMahon.

Joe MacKenna was very promising as a youngster but there would have been a query about his pace. He worked on that and it was not a problem when he became a senior. Anthony Daly only really flowered after he left Flannan's. He was a nice hurler and played on a Harty Cup winning side at corner-back, but if you were to pick three or four players, you wouldn't have picked Anthony at that time; yet, within two or three years, he had become one of the best young players in the country. One of his characteristics is his confidence. He's convinced that, no matter who's on him, he can mark him and beat him. He comes from a marvellous club, Clarecastle, with a fine tradition of coaching — probably started by a man called John Hanly, who did great work with them.

The curate's success at school level won him opportunities to take on new coaching challenges. In the mid-1980s he became involved with the Clare minors and later the under-21s, as well as the Ennis club Éire Óg. Then came the call to become a selector on the Clare senior hurling side.

Len Gaynor arrived as trainer in Autumn 1991, at a stage when morale in the county was at an all-time low. I was asked to become a selector when it was very hard to find anybody to agree to take the job. Morale was also very low among the players; in fact, my first job was to persuade Ger 'The Sparrow' O'Loughlin not to retire. I was involved with Len for a year and a half. Tony Kelly was a

Len Gaynor offers Bishop Walsh his analysis of a Clare performance.

*selector the first year, and when he dropped out Ger Loughnane succeeded him.
Then Ger and I stepped down for a year.*

*1992 was a significant year for Clare hurling, and in 1993 Clare got to the
Munster final, beating Cork and Limerick on the way, but they collapsed in
the final and lost to Tipperary by twenty points.'*

The match caused controversy in Clare when rumours spread about
the Tipperary dressing-room disparaging their opponents, but Bishop
Walsh feels that too much was read into the incident.

*I'd have to confess that I've made comments in dressing-rooms which I
wouldn't want repeated in public. When I was a manager or a mentor, one
thing I was always very careful about was saying something that could be used
in an opponent's dressing-room. The most famous example of this was Michael
Keating's comment that 'donkeys don't win derbies,' which was used very
skilfully by Fr Michael O'Brien to whip up the Cork boys before playing
Tipperary.*

Willie Walsh and Ger Loughnane were asked to return as selectors in
the autumn, and found the players still smarting after the Munster final
débâcle.

*The players felt humiliated by the scale of the defeat to Tipperary, so the whole
focus in 1994 was to beat Tipp in the Munster championship. We had a
meeting early on that year and agreed to do that, and we beat them by two
points. However, I always felt that we put so much effort into beating them
that we could never rise it again afterwards, and we collapsed against
Limerick in the Munster final.*

*I was appointed bishop during the Munster championship, so I had to step
aside as a selector, and after the Munster final Len Gaynor stepped down. Len
did a great job for Clare because he raised them from the floor, and in his time
we beat all the top teams in Munster, but we were never able to string a full
run of victories together. He was a great manager; I suppose he was the old-
style coach. It's only in recent years that counties like Tipperary and Cork
have gone in for coaching in a big way. I'll omit Kilkenny because they had Fr
Tom Maher, who was really the father of coaching in hurling.*

The appointment of Ger Loughnane as manager, however, was the
catalyst for the most successful era Clare hurling had ever seen.

*I've great admiration for someone like Justin McCarthy as a coach and a lover
of the skills of hurling, but I've no doubt that Ger Loughnane is the best coach
I've ever seen. He has a fantastic capacity to take a training session and get*

players to train very hard and at the same time enjoy it. Every training session is planned to the last minute, and it was always clear he knew what he was doing. He insisted that Clare hurling was too slow, that players weren't moving the ball fast enough and were playing at a slower pace than the top counties, and he reversed that. He brought in Mike McNamara, who did a great job on the physical side, and Tony Considine, a man totally committed to hurling.

We had a very fine bunch of players, who had distinguished themselves at under-21 and Fitzgibbon level, and great management, and all the pieces came together in 1995. We got the breaks that year with late goals against Cork and Offaly, but I feel the breaks went against us in 1996 and 1998. I don't think we could say that about 1999: of the six matches we played in the championship, we only deserved to win two of them. With the commitment that is required nowadays it is very hard to stay on top. Still, the whole scene has changed in Clare since 1995, and that can be seen in the great success we've had at club level since.

Bishop Walsh played his part in that success also, though the background role of the selector does not often receive such recognition. He recalls the ambiguous status of the selector with a wry anecdote:

One of the things that always struck me in hurling was the strange ways positional switches were made in a match. Straight away I think of the 1990 hurling final between Cork and Galway. I was wondering what the Cork selectors were going to do about Jim Cashman because Joe Cooney was destroying him, and when they went in at half-time I said, 'Well, Jim Cashman won't be centre-back in the second half.' Amazingly he was, and he went on to win his battle with Joe Cooney in the second half and Cork won the All-Ireland.

I went back to Clare and some people said to me, 'Ah, you can't beat those Cork guys. If that was Clare we'd have panicked and taken Jim Cashman off, but the Cork guys were wise and knew what was best.' Of course, that was a bit hurtful to me as a Clare selector, so I went down to Cork a month later and I went to Dr Con Murphy and I said, 'Up front, now, what happened with Jim Cashman and why didn't you change him?' And he replied, 'Well, we all agreed that Jim was being beaten and we'd have to change him: the problem was that none of the selectors could agree on who we would replace him with, so we decided to do the usual thing and give him five minutes in the second half.'

I remember in 1994 we were playing Tipperary and we were being beaten in midfield. Ger Loughnane wanted to bring Jamesie O'Connor centre-field but I felt if we did that we would be robbing Peter to pay Paul, because we had to get a few more points to beat Tipperary and Jamesie was the one forward who would do that for us. Ger Loughnane and myself were arguing on the sideline until eventually we called Len Gaynor over and both of us put our case to him. Len favoured Ger's option, so we made the switch. Within a few moments, Jamesie O'Connor had scored two points and lifted the whole team and we won the match. Afterwards everybody said, 'Ah, that was a great change ye made,' without knowing it was the toss of a coin. A match often hangs on a thing like that. The day it works you're a hero; the day it doesn't you're useless.

In 1998 Ger Loughnane sparked off a major controversy when he condemned the attitude of the authorities to the Banner county. What did Bishop Walsh think of the dispute? He says,

When things went wrong in 1998, some people would say Ger went over the top. Ger felt very strongly an injustice had been done in relation to Colin Lynch, but I suppose on reflection we might have lost our focus a little bit and spent too much time concentrating on the controversies surrounding Colin — though were it not for the enormous ill-luck of the All-Ireland semi-final, the year might have ended very differently for us. Ger was very involved emotionally. He saw his job as defending players, and he may have been inclined to see that if you didn't fully go along with what was being said you were being disloyal to players. I don't think that was completely fair.

The controversy was a very emotive subject in Clare and it was very divisive; you had to be on one side or the other. Obviously I'm in a very sensitive position: apart from being friendly with Ger I'm also friendly with Fr Seamus Gardiner. I was attacked coming out of Thurles by a fanatical Clare supporter because of Fr Seamus Gardiner's involvement in the Munster Council; he was in some way blaming me for what happened. It's still a very emotive and difficult subject to talk about in Clare.

The whole saga ended with great dignity because defeat was handled very graciously, and in 1999 Ger was very gracious in defeat also.

However, 1999 saw a new controversy erupt when a brawl broke out between the Tipperary and Clare camps at the Munster under-21 final. Rivalry between the two counties had given away to bad feeling. This was a source of deep concern to Bishop Walsh.

I think it's time for us in Clare and Tipperary to put the past behind us. There are, I think, difficulties in the relationship with Tipperary going back a number of years. There would be a feeling in Clare that Tipp hurling people looked down on them. There was always that sort of problem. Is it that Clare had an inferiority complex or because Tipperary were arrogant? It is very difficult to say.

The diocese of Killaloe, of which I'm bishop, straddles both counties. I'd be putting it to the players and managers in both counties that, whatever happened in the past, we have to end the bickering, because that's not what hurling is about. The tradition in hurling is that you bust your gut to win on the field, but after that it's over. I think that Clare need to end the idea that in some way other counties are against them.

Bishop Walsh is not a man to dodge awkward questions, though he baulked when asked to select his dream team.

Having looked at the centenary team, I think it's almost impossible to pick a dream team. Who would you pick at full-back? Brian Lohan? Pat Hartigan? Martin Doherty? If you were to look at the 1990s alone, however, you might be able to pick a team of the decade.

I would have Davie Fitzgerald in goal — though Cork people would insist on Ger Cunningham. I would go for Limerick's Steve McDonagh, one of the most underrated players of the last fifteen years, with Brian Lohan and Martin Hanamy as the full-back line. Sean McMahon would have to be centre-back with both Liam Doyle and Anthony Daly as strong candidates for the wing-back places; but of course Brian Whelahan would have to get a place, and where would you pick Ciaran Carey?

I'm not sure Tony Browne was around long enough at the top level to get a place at midfield, so I would go for Ollie Baker and Johnny Pilkington. I've great admiration for Johnny. I wish he minded himself a little better, but Johnny has his own theories about that. He's got an extraordinary capacity to turn up in the last few minutes and score a crucial goal. Gary Kirby is my centre-forward, which means that Martin Storey goes on the wing. Jamesie O'Connor and D.J. Carey both have to get places on the team. John Troy could slot in at full-forward. Nicky English and Pat Fox had probably their best days behind them in the 1990s, but is there a place for John Leahy? There were an awful lot of fine Galway players in the 1990s, and remember the Sparrow made a great contribution to Clare, as Johnny Dooley did for Offaly.

The life of a selector. Bishop Walsh adds a further thought.

I worked with a character in Ennis called Paddy Duggan, 'the Duggie' we used call him. Duggie's whole life was hurling. When he became ill I went to see him in hospital, and he had got the news that day that he only had a short time to live. He said, 'I'd like you to do the funeral Mass and make all the arrangements.' I agreed. Then he came back immediately: 'That's fine, Willie.

I still believe that we'd have won the county final last year if they'd listened to me at half-time.' As soon as the funeral was arranged he was straight back to the most important thing in life: hurling!

I'll never forget another incident with him. We were playing a club match and all of a sudden I saw this young lad, Tomás Fogarty, being introduced as a sub on our team. I was amazed and ran up the sideline to ask the secretary who had given the order to bring him on, and the secretary answered, 'Was it not you? The Duggie came up to me and said, "Fr Willie wants him in."'